Fig. 1 (*Frontispiece*).—Fichu and sleeve trimmings of old needle-point lace

NEEDLE-MADE LACES AND NET EMBROIDERIES

Reticella Work, Carrickmacross Lace,
Princess Lace and Other
Traditional Techniques

by

Doris Campbell Preston

DOVER PUBLICATIONS, INC.
NEW YORK

Published in Canada by General Publishing Company, Ltd., 30 Lesmill Road, Don Mills, Toronto, Ontario.
Published in the United Kingdom by Constable and Company, Ltd., 10 Orange Street, London WC2H 7EG.

This Dover edition, first published in 1984, is an unabridged and unaltered republication of the work first published by The Woman's Magazine Office, London, in 1938 under the title *Needle-Made Laces and Net Embroideries*.

Manufactured in the United States of America
Dover Publications, Inc., 31 East 2nd Street, Mineola, N.Y. 11501

Library of Congress Cataloging in Publication Data

Preston, Doris Campbell.
  Needle-made laces and net embroideries.

  Reprint. Originally published: London : Woman's Magazine Office, 1938.
  1. Needlepoint lace. 2. Netting. I. Title.
TT800.P9 1984   746.2'2   84-4207
ISBN 0-486-24708-2

TO

JUDITH SWEET

AND

HESTER DAWES

WHOSE INVALUABLE HELP AND

ENCOURAGEMENT MADE THIS

BOOK POSSIBLE

NOTE, 1984: The sections entitled "Materials" in each chapter occasionally contain specific references to 1938 prices and English sizes. Consult your local supplier for current particulars.

PREFACE

THE object of this book is to introduce to the reader
some types of lace-making and net embroidery which
she may hitherto have passed by. Lace-making has
so often been perched on a pedestal of tradition and
surrounded by an aura of sanctity that the average
needle-woman has hesitated to claim even its simplest
principles as her own.

My aim therefore is to deal with such methods as,
while characteristic of the old crafts, may be practically adapted to modern requirements. Aided by these
simple instructions, together with the diagrams and
photographs, it should be possible to gain a working
knowledge of each different type of the work. Having
accomplished this, the reader will be able to evolve
her own interpretations, thus adding to the sum total
of the world's beauty.

CONTENTS

CHAPTER   PAGE

     PREFACE 7

1. FROM THEN UNTIL NOW. AN INTRODUCTION . . 15

2. NEEDLE-RUN LACE 30

3. TAMBOUR LIMERICK 59

4. CARRICKMACROSS LACE 65

5. IRISH CROCHET 81

6. RETICELLA WORK 95

7. PRINCESS LACE 108

8. MODERN NEEDLE-POINT LACES 114

9. FILET LACE 127

10. TATTING 136

11. MODERN ADAPTATIONS OF NEEDLE-MADE LACES AND NET
     DARNING 148

12. THE CARE OF LACE 151

     GLOSSARY OF THE COMMONER LACE TERMS . . 157

     INDEX 158

9

ILLUSTRATIONS

PAGE

Fig. 1 Fichu and sleeve trimmings of old needle-point
lace   *Frontispiece*

Fig. 2 Wedding veil and dress flounce of Limerick lace   32

Fig. 3 A wedding veil in Isle of Wight lace   35

First set of diagrams (Limerick):
    I   Tent Stitch   42
    II Cobweb Stitch   42
    III Basket Stitch   44
    IV Herringbone Stitch   44
    V   Fancy Satin Stitch   45
    VI Satin Stitch Dots   46

Second set of diagrams (Limerick):
    VII Knotted Stitch   47
    VIII Detached Rings   48
    IX Buttonhole Filling   49
    X   Slanting Crossed Stitch   50
    XI Figure Eight Stitch   51
    XII Overcasting or Whipped Stitch   52

Fig. 4 Sampler A, showing a selection of needle-run stitch
groups   54

Fig. 5 Sampler B, showing a selection of needle-run stitch
groups   57

Fig. 6 Sampler C, showing the tambour stitch and finished
lace   63

Fig. 7 Mat in Carrickmacross Guipure   69

11

ILLUSTRATIONS

PAGE

Fig. 8   A handkerchief square in Carrickmacross Appliqué
and Guipure combined   71

Third set of diagrams (Carrickmacross):

    XIII   Method of fixing Carrickmacross   73
    XIV   A Figure Eight Stitch   74
    XV   Feather Stitch   75
    XVI   Simple Laced Stitch   75
    XVII   Buttonholed Bar for Guipure   76
    XVIII   Woven Leaf Vein for Guipure   77

Fig. 9   Sampler D, Carrickmacross Guipure needle-point
fillings   78

Fig. 10   Sampler E, specimens of Irish Crochet   86

Fig. 11   Some small Irish Crochet motifs, joined and edged 93

Fig. 12   Finished Reticella on a linen ground   96

Fig. 13   Sampler F, foundations for Reticella work   101

Fourth set of diagrams (Reticella):

    XIX   Close Buttonhole Filling   103
    XX   Whipped Bar   104
    XXI   Woven Bar   105
    XXII   Buttonhole Edging   105
    XXIII   Open Buttonhole Filling   106
    XXIV   Double-sided Buttonhole Bars   106

Fig. 14   Modern needle-point worked on laid threads   107

Fig. 15   Princess lace, showing borders of filled caskets 109

Fig. 16   Sampler G, arrangements of simple darning used in
Princess lace   111

Fig. 17   Braid Point, known as English Point, utilizing many
of the stitches shown on Sampler H   115

ILLUSTRATIONS

PAGE

Fig. 18 Some specimen braids and gimp edgings used in
Princess lace and English Point   117

Fifth set of diagrams (Point lace stitches):

    XXV Buttonhole Stitch   120

    XXVI Pyramid Stitch   120

    XXVII Wheel Stitch   121

    XXVIII A Veining Stitch   121

    XXIX Buttonholed Bar, with Thorn   122

    XXX A Twisted Filling Stitch   123

Fig. 19 Sampler H, showing a variety of needle-point stitches 124

Fig. 20 A square mat of filet lace   128

Sixth set of diagrams (Filet net):

    XXXI First position of the hands for making
filet net   131

    XXXII Second position of the hands for making
filet net   132

    XXXIII Third position of the hands for making
filet net   132

    XXXIV A finished square of filet net, before the
last two meshes are tied   134

Fig. 21 Sampler I, in large specimens, showing the principles
of Tatting   143

Seventh set of diagrams (Tatting):

    XXXVA First position of the hands   139

    XXXVB Second position of the hands   139

    XXXVI Third position of the hands   140

    XXXVII Fourth position of the hands   140

    XXXVIII Fifth position of the hands   141

    XXXIX Using two shuttles   144

Fig. 22A Small motifs and edgings in Tatting, taken from an 145
Fig. 22B old sampler   147

Fig. 23 Method of drying lace, showing the edges pulled out
on supporting pins   153

Eighth set of diagrams (Net mending):

    XL, XLI, XLII Net mending   156

CHAPTER I

FROM THEN UNTIL NOW
AN INTRODUCTION

In a practical handbook such as this it is impossible to enter fully into the history of the craft, especially such a controversial history as that of lace. Nevertheless, when acquiring the knowledge of any type of artistic or creative work it is tremendously interesting to have before one an outline, if only a slight one, of its ancestry and traditional characteristics. Although this book deals more with types of work that are based upon and take their name from lace than with lace itself, time will not be ill spent if for a moment we put the clock back and endeavour to link the romance of the past with the practical products of the present.

Embroidery and lace have always been so intermixed that it is wellnigh impossible to say where one begins and the other ends. It must therefore remain a matter for conjecture whether embroidery in the form of drawn threadwork was the forerunner of lace or whether lace-making was an independent craft evolved on an early form of net. There is romance in the picture of a very industrious Eve in the earliest ages of man adorning and improving upon the crude network that her husband had devised to simplify his fishing. For has it not always been a woman's work to beautify and turn to her own uses the utilitarian inventions of man? One admits there is little support for this theory. Only a few scrappets of what might be lace and net clinging to old garments of Egyptian or Coptic origin. Yet lack of evidence may well be due to the very perishable nature of such a fabric. You will have noticed how frail are the ancient textiles we treasure in our Museums. Even the closely woven pieces of comparatively thick thread will scarcely bear handling. What chance then would such gossamer threads as lace have against the ravages of time? No; lack of evidence need never persuade us to believe this beautiful work was unknown in some form or other in the marvellous ancient civilization of the East.

On the other hand there is abundant proof that a certain type of needle-made lace was evolved from embroidery. First a thread or series of threads was pulled out and either replaced with one of another colour or worked over in such a way as to form a pattern. As time went on the number of threads drawn was increased and the designs became more and more complicated. From this stage it was a short step to cut-work, when a part of the material was cut away and the space overlaid with threads on which a design was worked. It is only reasonable to suppose that this work grew into what is known as 'punto in aria', a very early form of lace-making executed with a needle as the phrase suggests 'in the air'. This was done by laying threads over a parchment and working upon them, so creating a fabric 'out of nothing'. When the work was complete the parchment was removed. The principle is used to-day in most forms of needle-point lace and from this very early beginning grew the exquisite point laces we all know and admire.

Although there are not many specimens of very early lace in a state of good repair, we have reliable records in the work of the Florentine Painters. They have perpetuated the intricate fine workmanship of the fifteenth century lace-makers in such perfect detail that in many paintings it is possible to discern the exact design.

As in most forms of ancient craft-work it is almost impossible to state the exact place of origin of lace-making as we know it to-day. Even in very early days people travelled, emigrated, were made prisoners of war, or brought home wives or servants from foreign countries. Such travellers as these on reaching the country of their adoption were only too anxious to pass on their knowledge to those around them. Soon their pupils became proficient and added new ideas of their own, either devising new stitches or introducing simpler methods. In many cases new methods followed the use of different materials more easily obtainable in the district. Although we find the earliest authentic record of lace in Italy, France and Spain are able to produce convincing evidence dating from about the same period. From these several starting-points lace-making soon spread throughout Europe. In this country consorts of foreign birth were largely responsible for teaching and popularizing the art. Anne of Bohemia, Katherine of Aragon and Mary of Scotland were all experts with the needle, and there

17

is little doubt were assiduous in instructing their ladies, who in their turn handed the knowledge on to their serving-women.

As each district or country adopted the craft new and original touches gave character and names to the work, thus producing the many varieties of lace we now know. Industries grew up to supply the practical requirements of the people and the dictates of fashion. Much of the work was done in the homes of the gentry and in the convents. Peeresses and peasants, artisans' wives, nuns, and even little children learned and practised the craft to satisfy an ever-growing demand.

There is no doubt that this demand was stimulated by that marvellous needle-woman and dictator of fashion, Catherine de Medicis. During her lifetime we might almost call it the lace age, for every country in Europe was producing needle-women and lace-makers of unrivalled ability, the exquisitely embroidered and lace-trimmed dresses of the period bearing witness to their skill. So much was spent on lace that in some countries, notably France, special laws had to be passed to check the unparalleled extravagance of the wealthy.

At this period all the lace was still entirely needle-made. Many of the designs were particularly lovely, for the artist and the craftsman were either one and the same person, or were working in a close alliance unusual at a later date. The stitchery was of miraculous fineness, often too fine for us to see with the naked eye. Those who study the early specimens have always found them a matter for wonder and amazement, remembering that modern aids to sight were unknown, and the indifferent lights, candle-stools or inadequate oil lamps, must have shortened the hours when working was possible. Nevertheless, there could not have been a more fascinating pastime in an age when leisure was unlimited.

Late in the sixteenth century a pillow lace made with bobbins appeared in Flanders, adding an entirely new branch to the industry. Since we are only dealing with needle-made laces we shall not follow this new method very closely, except to mention the fact that several products of the pillow and bobbin, such as Brussels ground, Honiton braids and edgings have been reproduced in recent years on a machine and are the basis of several modern needle-made laces.

We have only to look round our picture galleries and study our family portraits to see how the lace fashion fluctuated during the next few centuries. The great Elizabethans favoured it, the Puritans suppressed it, the Restoration revived it, and thereafter, like most other fashions, it came and went in cycles of popularity, but never quite disappeared from every-day life.

At one time lace-making represented the third largest industry in England. Some authorities attribute our well-known Honiton laces to the Huguenot refugees, while others maintain it was in existence at an earlier date; but wherever it originated it was made in considerable quantities in the villages of Devon and marketed from the town from which it takes its name. Buckingham laces, particularly the old specimens, are exceedingly beautiful in design and workmanship.

Up to the middle of the eighteenth century, lace had been divided into two groups: the pillow or bobbin laces, and the needle-point varieties. In a few cases the methods were combined in one lace, the braid, or sprays (toile) being made on the pillow, and the ground being added with the needle. As a general rule, however, one method or the other was used throughout.

The coming of machine-made net revolutionized the whole craft. Bobbin workers used the net as a mount for their motifs and needle-workers used it as a time-saving ground for their many lovely stitches. This enabled them to undertake much larger pieces of work, so that lace was made into whole garments and large hangings instead of only being used as a trimming.

It was in the late eighteenth century that a Nottingham man first attempted to make net on a stocking frame. From his small beginnings has developed the flourishing Nottingham lace industry now existing in that town. So far has the craft advanced and so perfect are some of the modern machine-made reproductions that it takes the eye of an expert to distinguish them from hand-made lace. In fact specimens have been exported to the Continent where an addition of a few handwork stitches has been made, and the work resold to this country as hand-made.

The first net was composed of a series of looped meshes such as one would expect from a stocking frame working on the knitting principle. There was a single thread running throughout the fabric. If this was broken or an attempt made to cut the edges of the net it unravelled and pulled out. The first mesh was of the type later known as Brussels ground. Other craftsmen working on the same principle produced other shaped meshes, but their nets still consisted of a single thread. An effort was made to consolidate the mesh with gum, but this was not really satisfactory. In a very short time other ingenious mechanics were busily working out new methods with the result that they obtained the locked mesh we now use.

After the perfecting of machine-made net by one John Heathcote came its adoption by the recognized lace industries. During the first few years machine-made net, with the design hand-darned, was more highly esteemed than lace wholly made by hand and it commanded quite as good a price. Later, bobbin-workers who made braided lace were inspired to try and lessen their own labour in a similar manner. Thus very soon braids, gimps and other units were made on the machine and afterwards modelled, joined and embellished by hand. It is from this mixture of machine and hand-work that our modern laces have grown, adapting themselves to our lessening leisure, less perfect eyesight and less nimble fingers.

Here we must say farewell to the laces of history, except to keep the beauty of them always in our minds as an inspiration. If we cannot hope to compete with the workmanship, we can at least help to perpetuate the lovely designs and effects. Surely it is better for us, as enthusiastic lace lovers, to do our small best to keep such lovely work alive, rather than let it die forgotten and crumbling to dust on our Museum shelves. Even if our leisure is scarce and our fingers less skilled than those of our ancestors I see no reason for this to discourage us, because modern methods have lightened our task in the quest for the beautiful. If, at times, we are tempted to adopt unconventional methods, can we not claim the same licence as the workers of old, who adapted their knowledge to their own limitations and let the result justify the means?

NEEDLE-RUN LACES

The first needle-run laces were originated in and about Nottingham very soon after the perfecting of machine-made net. Although this type of work has always been dignified by the name of lace it is in reality embroidery. The old patterns and many new ones were darned on the machine-made net and beautified with a number of decorative filling stitches. Many of these stitches were 'lifted' from drawn thread embroideries. Industries producing this type of lace were started in Limerick, the Isle of Wight and Coggershall, Essex. In these three centres the method was identical, but each district soon developed its own minor characteristics. Much of the Limerick lace was adorned with small dainty flower sprays, the well-shaped spaces between (caskets) being filled with fancy stitching. The designs used in the Isle of Wight were a bolder type, usually floral and utilizing the rose in one form or another. In this lace the filling stitches are more often employed within the designs, beautifying flower petals or leaves, or bold relief effects obtained by using close rows of plain darning.

Many needle-run stitches are common to all these laces, while others are peculiar to one district. In recent years the interchange of stitches and types of design has become more common, making the classifying of modern specimens exceedingly difficult.

This particular form of lace-making had a very profitable run of popularity during the reign of Queen Victoria when there was a vogue for lace dresses, flounces, trimmings, scarves, shawls, coatees, ladies' caps and other articles of clothing. Thus fashion gave the designer unlimited scope. It is therefore to be regretted that so many of the designs of this period were deplorably bad, most of the best work being in the traditional designs of a much earlier age.

Queen Victoria herself took a very great interest in these industries, especially that operating in the Isle of Wight. Several of her daughters had wedding dresses or veils made on the Island and many other pieces were commissioned for her own wardrobe. As the fashion changed the industry ceased to flourish and subsequent efforts to revive it failed until quite recently, when the Women's Institutes have done much to re-establish its popularity.

Limerick laces enjoyed a longer prosperity. First taken to Ireland in the early 'fifties, by an Oxford man, they gave employment to upwards of 1,500 people. In that country another method of outlining the design was introduced, known as Tambour. This is composed of a series of chain stitches worked with a hook in the manner of a crochet chain into the net mesh. Some of the Limerick laces were entirely made with this stitch, others combined it with needle-run filling stitches, while others again retained the old method of darning in the outline. After the perfecting of machine-made lace the tambour method was so easily and beautifully copied that it fell into disuse amongst the hand-workers who returned to their original method of running the outline.

Unlike other Irish lace industries, most of which were started by philanthropic ladies, and not run for profit, the Limerick lace was for some time a paying concern. Unfortunately the quality of the products deteriorated so badly that the lace fell out of favour for a time. But at the beginning of this century the work was successfully revived, largely owing to the enthusiastic workers who made a special effort to improve not only the design and material but also the workmanship. At the present time the largest industry for making needle-run lace is in Southern India, where it was carried by those interested in the welfare of the native women, and observant of their extraordinary ability in doing this kind of embroidery.

CARRICKMACROSS LACE

Carrickmacross lace traces its origin back to 1820 and is the oldest of the Irish laces. It was first copied from specimens of Italian lace by Mrs. Grey Porter and her maid-servant, Mary Steadman. The skill of the latter was so great that her fame soon spread and others were interested to learn the craft. Eventually

Miss Reid, of Rahans, near Carrickmacross, started an industry which flourished for some years.

Carrickmacross lace is of two kinds, Guipure and Appliqué. The Guipure variety has a design worked out in muslin and joined with needle-point bars and stitches. The appliqué lace is worked on a net ground, the appliqué being of muslin, either button-holed or overstitched into place. In this lace the filling stitches are similar to those used in Limerick lace.

IRISH CROCHET

Before leaving Ireland we must just touch on their exquisite crochet and Reticella work. Irish crochet was first made about the year 1846 by one Mademoiselle Riego de la Blanchardière. This lady, having made a study of a certain very beautiful type of Spanish needle-point, set out to copy it with her crochet hook. The results were astonishingly lovely and created a very widespread interest amongst her friends and acquaintances.

During the great Irish Potato Famine the gentle-women of the country taught lace-making, and marketed the work to enable the peasantry to gain a meagre living. It was at this time that Irish crochet, like most other Irish laces, became a national industry.

Although the principles of the work are the same as those used in modern crochet, the creative worker will find it much more suitable for individual inter-pretation. As the design is built up from a series of motifs, later joined with crochet bars, it lends itself to different arrangements better than our flat continuous modern designs that are worked in one piece.

RETICELLA WORK

Reticella lace is one of the oldest forms of needle-point and the root from which most of the other point laces have grown. It has been selected as being a good illustration to demonstrate the method and stitches common to all point laces, and being a coarser work than most, these will be more easily followed and learnt.

Largely owing to its delightfully modern geometrical designs Reticella work is returning to favour, but the modern needle-woman has adopted a labour-saving base of drawn thread linen in place of the old method of laid threads, thus returning to the old cut-work method from which it is probable that the lace originally sprang.

ENGLISH POINT AND MODERN POINT LACES

Devonshire or English Point is one of the most popular of modern laces. The base of the work is the beautiful machine-made copies of bobbin-made braids such as are used in Honiton and Brussels laces.

The braids are tacked on to a parchment bearing the design and the spaces are filled and the joins made with needle-point stitches and bars such as those used in Reticella and other point laces.

One of the charms of this work is its infinite variety.

The same design embellished with different filling stitches or made up with different braids can produce two totally dissimilar pieces of work.

PRINCESS LACE

Princess lace might almost be called the connecting link between the point and needle-run laces, as both methods are combined, point braids being appliquéd on to a net ground and fillings worked in either point or needle-run stitches. In France this type of work is often called Renaissance Work, and the same term is applied to English Point. The work is very simple and for this reason should recommend itself to the beginner.

FILET LACE

Filet lace is probably the most popular generally useful product of the modern lace-maker. Although it has its beginnings in a very early past, being mentioned in old Jewish records and frequently in documents of the early Courts, it has, however, kept up with the times, being adapted to modern requirements by both hand-workers and machinists. The square hand-made mesh can be of any size, making it suitable for any article from a coarse curtain to a gossamer hand-kerchief. The plain clear-cut darning of the design gives something of the squared effect of cross stitch. Although we are most familiar with the white or string-coloured versions, some of the specimens made during the last century show some very pleasing colour effects in both silk and wool.

TATTING

While dealing with so many lacy fabrics it seems impossible to exclude Tatting, especially in view of the fact that it is rapidly returning to favour.

Perhaps we associate this delightful work most closely with our grandmothers and great-grandmothers, who are said to have adopted the craft because it enabled them to show off the beauty of their hands. But the same work appearing under different names is of much more ancient origin. We find exactly the same methods applied in the 'Occhi' of Italy, the 'Makouk' of the Eastern world, and the delightful French 'Frivolité'.

Made with a shuttle and thread the finest specimens of Tatting resemble the most delicate laces, and considering that the stitch is composed of one double knot and its very limited variations it is amazing how wide a range of designs can be obtained.

MODERN ADAPTATIONS

It has already been suggested that the worker should adapt these authentic methods of lace-making to her own needs and present fashions. This book would not, therefore, be complete without some suggestions as to how this can be done. During the last few years many unconventional and daring needle-women have

28

modernized the work with really lovely and practical results. Such simple fabrics as squared curtain net and embroidery linen have been beautified beyond all belief, and some of the exquisite new colour ranges in silks and cottons have been utilized to gain glorious colour effects. Although in most cases only darning stitches have been used there is no reason why the work should not be further extended to include all the needle-run and needle-point stitches that lent to the original work such infinite variety and charm.

CARE OF LACE

There are those of us who admire and treasure specimens of rare old lace and it is for these primarily that a last small chapter is added on the care of this precious possession. Properly treated these delicate fabrics will last and wear for many years, but they are too often neglected and allowed to rot through want of a little knowledge.

This little knowledge can also be applied to modern laces of your own making which will last much longer if treated with the respect due to a work of art.

CHAPTER II

NEEDLE-RUN LACE

UNDER this heading are included Limerick run lace, Coggershall lace, and Isle of Wight lace, all of which are made in exactly the same way on the same principle.

METHOD OF WORKING

A machine-made net is stretched evenly over a parchment or cambric background bearing a very clear outline of the design. This, showing up clearly through the net, is then darned in by the simple process of threading the needle under and over the bars. As far as possible the thread should pass in and out of every mesh. If this is not consistent with keeping to the exact outline, as when rounding a curve, a mesh should be missed. The finer the mesh, the easier to keep the correct outline in conjunction with perfectly even darning. When the whole design is thus traced on the net it is ready to be embellished with filling stitches.

There are two ways of fixing this type of work; either is correct. Of these the individual must make her own choice. The first method is to use an embroidery frame. It should be of the large, square, sectional variety, with screw stretchers. The net must be mounted with the utmost care in the following manner. The horizontal bars of the frame are fitted with strong webbing bands on to which are stitched the upper and lower edges of the net. It is advisable to turn the edges of the net under so that it is double where stitched. This will prevent undue strain on the mesh. For the same reason the stitches which attach the mesh to the webbing should be even and fairly close together. If working on a long piece of fabric, say for a dress flounce, the surplus length should be carefully rolled up on the bottom roller after the preliminary fixing. The embroidery is then commenced at the top and carried toward the bottom roller. As each section is completed the stretcher bars are removed and the finished work rolled on to the upper roller and a fresh length of net released from the bottom. When the net has been rolled and adjusted to the length of the stretcher bars the side edges should be arranged and stitched between folded bands of cambric or muslin about 2 to 3 inches deep. The stretcher bars are now inserted and the screws tightened until there is an even pull on the net from top to bottom between the horizontal bars. Next, with a very strong long thread lace the sides of the net over the stretchers, taking the needle into the folded strips of material. These stitches should be placed fairly close together to take an equal strain. Before finishing off pull up the threads with the fingers one at a time until the tension is even and taut throughout. If necessary, tighten the stretcher screws slightly. The whole of this operation should be undertaken with great care as the ultimate success of the work depends much on getting an even

Fig. 2.—Wedding veil and dress flounce of Limerick lace

tension in all directions and so pulling the meshes into their correct shape.

We are now ready for the design. This should be stamped or traced on well-dressed cambric, waxed linen or parchment, or any other material which the point of the needle will not easily penetrate during working. Ready-prepared designs can be purchased from reputable fancy-work departments. Of the preparation of original designs there is more to be said anon.

Assuming the design to be in order it is placed in the correct position under the net. A few pins may be used to hold it in place until it is properly tacked, but these must all be removed before starting work or they will become hopelessly entangled with the thread, causing infinite trouble. The tacking should be close and thorough, as any slipping apart of the two fabrics during working will ruin the design. One or two points require special attention. The tacking needle should never on any account split a bar. If this is done the net will be dragged at this point and often the bar will break; at best the mesh will become misshapen. Neither should the tacking thread ever be allowed to cross the outline of the design on the upper side of the work, or it may be stitched in with the outlining thread which will be pulled out of place when the tackings are removed. For the same reason no tacking thread should cross a space where filling stitches are to be used.

The second method of fixing the work is the same in principle but does away with the use of a frame; a great advantage if the worker wishes to pack or carry the work easily, and much less tiring to handle.

As before the design should be arranged on a stiffish background, pale-blue waxed linen is best, as this is very firm and the colour prevents undue eyestrain. The net in this case is tacked directly over the parchment, but there being no firm frame the stretching of the mesh is only such as can be done with the tacking thread. Special care is therefore required to keep it a good shape. The few points mentioned as needing attention in the first manner of fixing apply equally to this method.

After these preliminaries we come to the actual embroidery. The main factor in success is keeping an even tension on the thread throughout. This specially applies when rounding a curve or an angle. Should the thread become too tight or too slack the ultimate beauty of the work will be quite spoilt. With a little practice the correct tension is easily acquired.

As we have already seen, the outlining of the design in Limerick run lace, Coggershall and Isle of Wight is entirely darned. This is so simple that it needs no further explanation, except to stress the point that the whole design or section of the design should be outlined before any filling stitches are worked, and to note that the thread used for the outline is more effective if it is considerably thicker than that used for the fillings. If any difficulty is experienced the stitch is best practised on a coarse net in coloured thread. Any defect is then at once seen and checked. This method is excellent for learning the more difficult filling stitches.

Fig. 3.—A wedding veil in Isle of Wight lace

If a stitch is composed of two rows these would be worked in different colours, showing clearly the direction which each thread should take. As soon as the rhythm is learned by heart it is easily adapted to a mesh of any shape or size, or incorporated in a group of other stitches.

There is, as one might suppose, a right and wrong way to thread the needle. The thread should be doubled and the two ends passed through the eye of the needle. Pass the thread under the first mesh and through the looped end, thus holding it fast round the bar. It is usual to work the outline with a double thread and use a single thread for the filling stitches. A single thread is commenced with a minute knot made over the bar and both single and double threads may be finished in this way, or alternatively, they may be run under the outline for a short distance. When working filling stitches always ascertain if there is enough thread to finish the row, as a join should not be made in the middle of a space. Whichever method of finishing is used the thread should be cut off close to the outline. There is still much to be said about filling stitches, but these we will learn as we require them, with the assistance of diagrams and samplers.

DESIGNS

Now, having seen exactly what we intend to do, and the general principles to be followed, we are in a position to choose suitable materials and designs. Perhaps it is wiser to decide upon the latter first, as this will have considerable bearing on our choice of materials.

Above all, a design should be good. That is, it should be pleasing, simple, and satisfying in line, and suitable for the purpose for which it is intended. In a lace design, as much attention should be given to the space between the units as to the actual units themselves, for it is these spaces which if well-shaped look so lovely when embellished with filling stitches. Many Art Needlework shops carry a good stock of designs for all kinds of lace, but of late the demand has not been very great. It may therefore be difficult to get exactly what is required to suit a given purpose.

It is quite easy to arrange one's own designs and so make sure of satisfactory results. The best source of inspiration is old lace, many of the old designs being particularly beautiful. If a good specimen can be obtained it may be pinned out flat and the design traced or pricked on a thin tracing paper. The first method will only give a rough outline as the bumps in the pattern will break the line. The drawing must therefore be corrected where necessary and retraced on to waxed linen or parchment. The final tracing should be strongly outlined in ink.

To prick a design, spread the tracing paper over the lace and follow the outline closely with a line of pin-pricks made in the paper. If necessary, this may be darkened with a pencil line to facilitate the final tracing on to the parchment. It is not essential that a design should be taken from the same type of lace as that about to be made. Many lovely results can be gained

37

by using other varieties with very little alteration. For instance, if working from Guipure Carrickmacross to make a design for Limerick needle-run the unnecessary brides would be omitted, the outline of the sprays only being used. Old pieces of embroidery also lend themselves excellently for building up designs.

Modern transfers are often quite suitable, especially those arranged for braiding or cut-work. Here again the unwanted parts should be cut away before the final tracing is completed.

In the case of a transfer it may be stamped on the background in the usual way, but should the ground be of waxed linen, only a cool iron should be used, or the surface will be spoilt. If this does not give a dark enough line it may be inked over in the same way as a tracing.

If the lace is to be made without a frame a good margin should be left on the parchment, so that it may act as a guide when fixing the net. When preparing a tracing for an all-round border pattern it is only necessary to draw one corner and a quarter of a side so as each section is completed the design is removed and retacked under the next stretch of net. Care is needed during this operation to see that the design joins up correctly and neatly. If the edges of the parchment and the net edge are cut perfectly straight it will greatly help as they can then be arranged edge to edge, thus bringing the border on to the correct line of mesh.

When making small articles, such as cuffs, yokes or collars, the pattern should be cut out in the backing.

38

If turnings are required these should be added, but an ink line should be used to indicate the exact pattern size. The design is then traced within the allotted space. A square of net is fixed over the foundation as before. It is advisable to darn in the pattern shape with a coarse tacking thread to give a correct shape for cutting the pattern when the net is removed from the background. Having prepared a good design and outlined it the worker can use filling stitches in any way she pleases.

MATERIALS

Materials for this work should always be of the best, otherwise they will quickly show signs of wear and much time will have been wasted on fine stitchery worthy of a better fate. In any case the price of the materials is negligible. A few pence, or at most a shilling or two, will buy the necessary equipment for making a piece of lace worth pounds.

The net is the first consideration. This may be obtained in meshes of various shapes and sizes. Diamond-meshed Brussels net is much used in these laces. It may be had in white or cream, in various widths up to two yards, the widest is suitable for wedding veils and other large pieces of work.

Another popular medium, obtainable in the same widths, is the octagonal meshed net used by the Indian needle-run lace-makers. This has a specially strong bar and a neat close mesh which keeps its shape well during working. There are several good French nets, also, on the market. A selection is usually available at any good needlework shop, or lace department, or can be obtained together with the necessary threads from one of the several lace schools in the country. When purchasing a length of net it should be carefully inspected for flaws as these usually turn out to be weak spots. Even if this is not the case they spoil the beauty of the work.

The ideal thread is of softest flax. It works smoothly and wears wonderfully. It is supplied in large or small hanks. A really good stranded cotton is a very excellent substitute used by many workers. The results are most satisfactory, and the slight sheen on the thread adds lustre to the work.

According to the size of the net mesh, two or three strands are used for outlining the design, and one or two for filling stitches. If two are used for fillings they must be worked in separately.

Ordinary sewing needles—rather fine but not too short—and a pair of small embroidery scissors or lace scissors complete the equipment.

Some people finish the edges of the lace with a machine-made picot braid or pearl edging, others prefer to turn in the edge of the net ever so slightly and finish it with a tiny buttonholing. Either is correct.

Before commencing this work it is advisable to remove anything that might snag the net such as a ring with a claw setting, a rough thimble, or a 'catchy' buckle.

FILLING STITCHES

It is the filling stitches in their infinite variety that give character to this type of lace. In needle-run Limerick they are freely used and there seems no end to the diversity of grouping. A few basic stitches are shown in the diagrams, which illustrate clearly how each is worked. From the stitch samplers may be seen some of the ways in which they may be combined in groups of two or more to form fillings for different sized caskets.

DIAGRAM I. *Tent Stitch*

On this stitch several others are based. It may be worked diagonally or horizontally; alternatively it may be worked in one direction and then back, the second row of stitches crossing those of the first. In each case the result looks quite different. This stitch may be worked from right to left, or left to right, as is most convenient. Start at one end of a row and take a stitch, passing the needle over and down under the top bar of a mesh, and under and over the bottom bar of the next mesh. Another variation is to take the thread across each mesh, passing the needle under both top and bottom bars of the same mesh.

DIAGRAM II. *Cobweb Stitch*

This is a delightful stitch and when once mastered is quite easy. It is particularly effective used alone rather than in a stitch group. Two rows worked as shown in the diagram are necessary to complete the

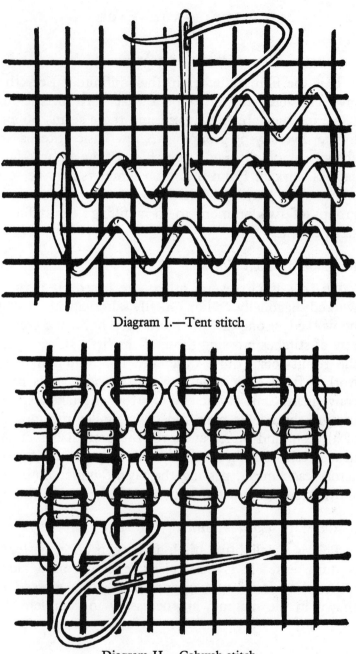

Diagram I.—Tent stitch

Diagram II.—Cobweb stitch

design. Starting from the left and working to the right, pass the needle under two bars and one mesh, bringing the cotton down slant-wise over two bars and a mesh and putting the needle in one bar back. Repeat the first stitch, then take the cotton up slant-wise over two bars and a mesh. Repeat these four stitches in a straight row. For the second row, turn the work and come back, making the bottom stitch of the top row lie side by side in the same mesh with the top stitch of the bottom row.

DIAGRAM III. *Basket Stitch*

This stitch can be worked either up, down or across the mesh, and may be in short blocks over one or two meshes or in a stretch of any length. The daintiest and prettiest effect is obtained by working on three meshes and four bars, or two meshes and three bars.

Pass the needle under and over a set of bars. In working back, take the thread under where it went over in the first row. Repeat this operation three or four times in the same meshes, thus making a solid block of woven stitching. These blocks may be repeated at right-angles round a centre mesh to form little stars. Alternatively the same stitch can be worked down a number of meshes, each line forming the side of a square.

The top right-hand corner of Sampler A, 4 illustrates the stitch used in a continuous straight line.

DIAGRAM IV. *Herringbone Stitch*

If worked in a straight line this stitch is very attrac-

43

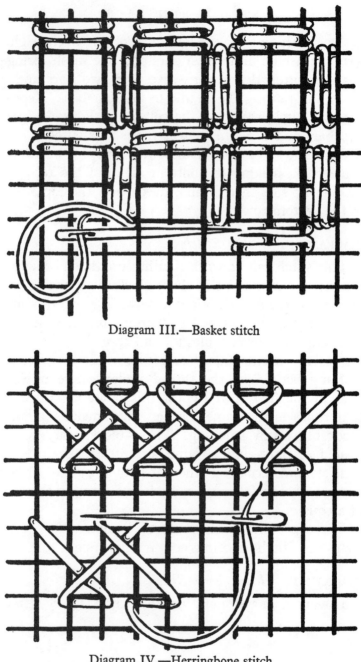

Diagram III.—Basket stitch

Diagram IV.—Herringbone stitch

tive for a border. It covers two meshes and three bars in exactly the same way as an ordinary herringbone stitch is worked in embroidery. The method is the same on any shaped mesh, but the effects are rather different. The stitch may be carried in any direction up, down or across the net from corner to corner.

DIAGRAM V. *Satin Stitch Stars*

Here is a very useful stitch as it can be used in so many ways. The tiny stars may be arranged in a bunch

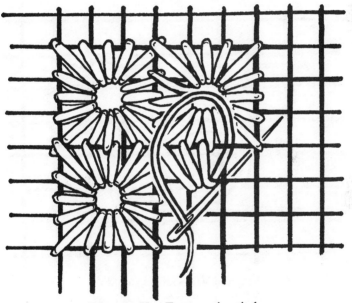

Diagram V.—Fancy satin stitch

as shown in the diagram, or they can in conjunction with another stitch form a centre motif (Sampler A, 2).

Starting from a centre mesh, knot the thread over

45

a bar and work one stitch into each of the surrounding meshes. If the stars are not too widely spaced the thread may be taken from one to the other behind the bars. If this appears too obvious each star must be finished off separately.

DIAGRAM VI. *Satin Stitch Dots*

A dainty little stitch this, that can be used either in rows, blocks, or as single dots. It consists of three or four satin stitches, worked across a single mesh. The

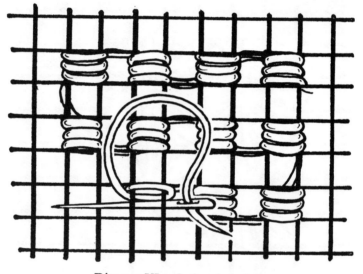

Diagram VI.—Satin stitch dots

number of stitches depends upon the size mesh they are required to fill. As in Diagram V the thread may be taken from group to group behind the mesh unless this appears unsightly.

DIAGRAM VII. *Knotted Stitch*

Like the simple snail trail used in embroidery this
stitch is worked on the net mesh. It is most effective
used in stitch groups, alternately with another stitch
as in Sampler A, 3.

Diagram VII.—Knotted stitch

Insert the needle slant-wise from left to right under
two bars and a mesh. Pass the thread under the point
of the needle from left to right and draw the thread
up into a knot. These are repeated down a row of
mesh working from the top to the bottom.

47

DIAGRAM VIII. *Ring Stitch*

Here is another stitch that can be used in several ways. Single rings make excellent centres for squares and diamonds formed by other stitches. Alternatively the stitch can be worked in rows, either detached or interlocked as in Sampler A, 4.

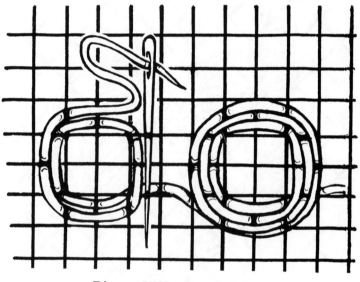

Diagram VIII.—Detached rings

Take four centre meshes or in the case of a tiny ring one centre mesh, and work three times round this space, darning under and over the bars of the surrounding meshes. The rings may be connected by passing the thread behind the bars or, if more convenient, may be finished off separately.

48

DIAGRAM IX. *Buttonhole Stitch*

This stitch is used in so many ways it is not possible in a limited space to illustrate them all. It is worked in exactly the same way as an embroidered buttonhole stitch. The diagram shows it worked in graduated points up and down the mesh. These points may be

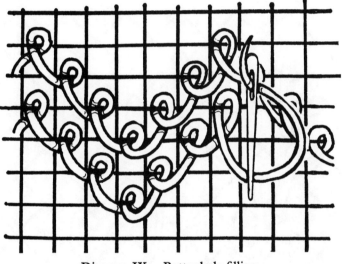

Diagram IX.—Buttonhole filling

of any length, regulated by the number of meshes used on the upward and downward grades. The same stitch is used in Limerick dots, Sampler A, 5, a very common filling in both needle-run and Tambour laces. In the latter lace the dots are worked in the Tambour chain, Sampler C, 4. In the case of the former the buttonhole stitch is worked round a centre mesh and finished off with the usual tiny knot.

49

One also sees buttonholing used in lines, squares and diamonds, and it is a very common method of finishing the edges of all darned net laces.

DIAGRAM X. *Slanting or Horizontal Crossed-stitch*

This is a very favourite stitch in Limerick lace. It is rather more difficult to follow than some, but when

Diagram X.—Slanting crossed-stitch

once mastered is simple enough and very effective. It consists of a figure eight stitch, worked horizontally across a diamond mesh (see movement A, Diagram X). The needle is then brought out at the bottom point of the diamond and taken straight up across the middle of the figure eight, and in at the top point. It should be brought out again under the left-hand point of the next diamond in readiness for the next figure eight stitch.

DIAGRAM XI. *Figure Eight Stitch*

This stitch rather resembles the last. It consists of a figure eight worked vertically in a zig-zag on a

Diagram XI.—Figure eight stitch

diamond mesh, and is interlaced with a second row of stitches similar to that shown in Diagram II. First work a row of figure eight stitches going from right to left, up and down, as shown in the diagram. Interlace a single row of cobweb stitch from left to right, but notice that with the changed shape of mesh the head of the stitch passes under four bars. This is shown quite clearly in Diagram XI, where the thread of the second row has been shaded to distinguish it from that of the first.

DIAGRAM XII. *Overcasting or Whipped Stitch*

Here is one of the simplest stitches, but when used

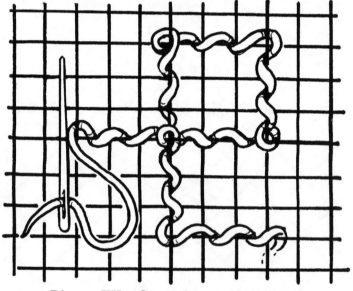

Diagram XII.—Overcasting or whipped stitch

in conjunction with others is very effective and quick for filling large caskets. Any size group of squares may be selected and outlined with whipping. The diagram shows one stitch in each mesh, but two or even three may be used in a large mesh if a thicker outline is required. It may also be used effectively in straight lines placed either horizontally or vertically.

Pierced holes as in Sampler A, 5, are made by stretching a mesh with a stiletto or knitting-pin as far as possible without breaking the thread and working the hole round with this stitch.

Samplers A and B will give some idea of the grouping of these stitches as used in needle-run laces, but the worker will find a number of other variations on existing specimens of this work and will, I am sure, devise many other arrangements for herself.

Sampler A

Worked on an octagonal mesh, this Sampler is divided into six caskets. A, 1, shows two arrangements of tent stitch (see Diagram I). The rows are worked diagonally in both directions. From left to right five meshes are left between the rows and from right to left the top corner shows one mesh between the rows and the bottom corner two and one meshes alternately.

Casket A, 2, shows a similar arrangement of tent stitch, but five meshes are left between the rows in both directions, so forming a series of diamonds. In each of these is worked a small satin stitch star (see Diagram V).

Casket A, 3. The filling shows diagonal rows of knot stitch (see Diagram VII), the upper part of the casket being filled with double rows of this stitch, alternating with rows of herringbone (see Diagram IV).

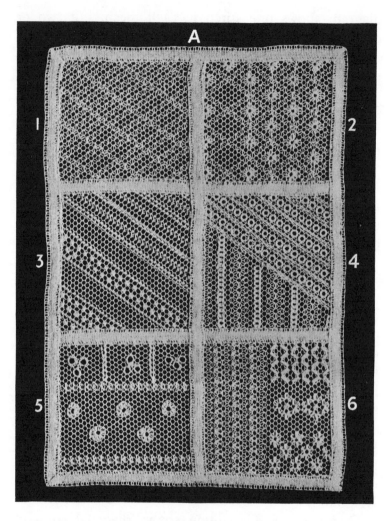

Fig. 4.—Sampler A, showing a selection of needle-run stitch
groups

54

The wider rows of knot stitch are worked on the outer edges of a mesh, the narrow rows on the inner edge. The bottom left-hand corner of the casket illustrates single rows of knot stitch bordering a double row of satin stitch dots (see Diagram VI), thus forming wide stripes suitable for filling large spaces.

Casket A, 4. Shown in the top corner are diagonal rows of a ring stitch (see Diagram VIII) separated by rows of basket or woven stitch (see Diagram III).

The vertical rows in the bottom left-hand corner of this space are of interlocked ring stitch in which the second ring is worked through the centre mesh of the first instead of into the adjoining mesh. These rows are alternated with a double row of cobweb stitch (see Diagram II).

Casket A, 5. Here are shown two small characteristic stitches often used to sprinkle a large background space. At the top are pierced holes, worked in threes, as described in the instructions for whipped stitch (Diagram XII). The bottom part of the casket is sprinkled with Limerick dots as described in buttonhole stitch (Diagram IX).

Casket A, 6. This space is devoted to the use of satin stitches in several different forms. The vertical lines on the left show a single row of cobweb stitch (Diagram II), with half a satin stitch star (Diagram V) worked from the centre of each stitch, one stitch only being taken into each surrounding mesh. The three groups on the right-hand side of the casket show other arrangements of satin stitch with two or three threads worked into each surrounding mesh.

Sampler B

Worked on a square mesh, also contains six caskets.

Casket B, 1. Illustrates an arrangement of button-hole stitch (see Diagram IX). Where the design forms a diamond, four meshes are darned into a solid block with basket stitch (Diagram III).

Casket B, 2. Here is shown the double eight stitch of Diagram XI worked in diagonal rows. The inter-twined stitch shown in the diagram with a darker thread is omitted.

Casket B, 3. The small squares in this pattern are of whipped stitch (Diagram XII) with a satin stitch dot (Diagram VI) in the centre of each square.

Casket B, 4. Here is a pretty arrangement of hori-zontal cross stitch (Diagram X). A row of this stitch is alternated with a row of darned rings or 'beads', in the centre of each being a single horizontal cross-stitch.

Caskets B, 5 *and B*, 6. In these two spaces are illus-trated the amazingly different effects that can be gained by using the same simple stitch in different ways. The stitch is worked diamond-wise on the net. The first movement of the needle goes from right to left under the top point of a diamond, and the next stitch goes from left to right under the side point of the same diamond. These stitches are repeated in a straight row as illustrated in the bottom left-hand corner of B, 6. The variations of the stitch are worked as follows. In the top right-hand corner of B, 5 it is worked in the same way but on a diamond shape consisting of four meshes. When the first row is complete, turn the work

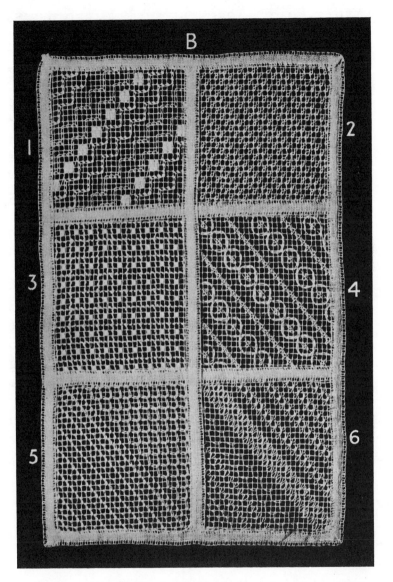

Fig. 5.—Sampler B, showing a selection of needle-run stitch groups

and come back over the same line of meshes making the looped stitch over the straight stitch and taking the straight stitch under the loops of the first row.

The bottom corner of this casket shows the stitch worked on one diamond mesh. Single rows are alternated with double rows of the same stitch. Either of these rows may be effectively used alone, the single stitch giving a light trellised effect and the double row a neat firm ground similar to continuous rows of double knot stitch.

B, 6, shows three arrangements of the foundation stitch simply illustrated. It is exactly the same in each case, but worked upon a different number of meshes. In the top corner of this space is a further arrangement in which the stitch is worked under the top point of the first mesh and the bottom point of the next. This stitch crossed is very effective. It may also be interlocked by working from left to right, taking the stitch of the second row under the point of the mesh which appears between the loop stitches of the first row. This throws the loop stitch of the second row one diamond point beyond the plain stitch of the first row, thus giving a lacy effect.

CHAPTER III

TAMBOUR LIMERICK

THIS method of outlining is not nearly so popular with the hand-workers as once it was, because of late it has been so freely copied in the cheapest of machine-made products. The general principles pertaining to needle-run laces apply also to this variety. The outline is composed entirely of very small chain stitches worked with a small hooked needle like a tiny crochet hook. Sometimes the whole design is outlined and filled with the same stitch. In other pieces variations of the chain stitch are found, or alternatively needle-run fillings are used.

MATERIALS

The nets used for needle-run lace are also suitable for tambour, but as the stitch is worked with a continuous thread as in crochet, the flax or cotton must be bought on reels. These are obtainable at most needlework shops in 250- or 200-yard lengths. A single thread only is used. The needles should be of the right gauge for the net selected or the stitch will not be nice and even. The best needles are adjustable. A fine crochet hook may be used as a substitute.

FIXING

The preliminary fixing of the net is done much as previously described.

A frame must be used in order to give the free use of both hands. The work is stretched in this, and the design prepared in the same way as for Limerick. The older schools advocate working the thread from the under side of the net. This necessitates leaving the design loose, tacking the top only. The worker is thus enabled to work with the left hand below the net and the right above. The design is lifted into place from time to time and a part of the design memorized.

The quicker and more modern method is to work with both thread and hook on the upper side of the net. The design can then be firmly tacked throughout as for needle-run. An alternative method is to work with a blunt-pointed needle working a chain stitch over each mesh. The stitch in either case is identical, so the worker can adopt whichever method comes easier to her.

When using a hook the thread may be worked continuously running off a reel. It is therefore necessary to prevent this rolling about and getting tangled. To do so thread a string through the centre hole of the reel, and tie it to the edge of the frame. Unwind a few feet of thread, and then put a wedge in the hole to prevent the reel turning until a fresh length of thread is required. A short piece of wood or a short knitting-pin will serve the purpose.

When the net is fixed and everything in readiness to

begin, set the frame in a good light. If the old method is being adopted it is a good plan to put a dark-blue or green cloth over the table in such a way that it forms a good background to show up the mesh.

The thread is then controlled from the under side with the left hand and crocheted up with the hook held in the right hand above the net. The left hand is also responsible for lifting the design from time to time in order that the next section may be memorized.

Following the more modern method the thread is still controlled with the left hand and the hook with the right, but both hands are above the net. The stitch is the same, one bar being taken in with each chain as the outline of the design is closely followed.

If using a needle and thread the latter cannot be run off a reel, therefore a long length must be broken off. The stitch is worked exactly as a chain stitch in embroidery. The start and finish of each thread must be made with a neat close knot tied round a bar. This must be particularly firm as should it work loose the whole chain will pull out.

The beginner sometimes has difficulty in making her two hands respond to different movements simultaneously, but quite considerable speed is gained with a little practice.

When the outline is complete the filling is either done with a few added rows of the same stitch or with one of its variations as shown in Sampler C. Alternatively one of the heavier needle-run stitches may be used, the lighter ones being too insignificant with the thicker outline.

61

The lace should be kept in the frame until it is quite complete. The edges may be finished in one of three ways. It is quite permissible to cut the net along the outer row of stitching. If the tambour is well worked this does not pull out unduly, but it requires no great reasoning power to form the opinion that a firmer method is better. Either the edge may be worked with a tiny, almost invisible, buttonhole stitch, or a very fine machine-made picot edging may be neatly run under the outer stitching after the edge has been cut.

Sampler C

Owing to the fact that tambour stitch is the same throughout merely varied by working it in different directions on the mesh, a drawn diagram has been discarded in favour of a stitch sampler which will give a better idea of the actual effects.

Casket C, 1. This shows a small piece of outlining in tambour stitch. It is worked on very coarse net to enable the worker to see the stitch clearly.

Casket C, 2. Here the same stitch is worked as a filling. Straight lines of tambour are alternated with wavy lines working up and down three meshes in each direction. The beaded effect in the same casket is obtained by working a second wavy line interlocked with the first.

Casket C, 3. Illustrates two more arrangements of the same stitch. The top section gives a zig-zag line, the stitch being taken from the top of one mesh to the bottom bar of the next and up again from bottom to top. A line of mesh should be missed between each row.

Fig. 6.—Sampler C, showing the tambour stitch and finished lace

The bottom section shows a cluster stitch. Four straight stitches, then a little cluster of six stitches, taken round a centre mesh. The seventh stitch is worked into the centre mesh from which the next straight line begins.

Casket C, 4. The top section of the casket contains another zig-zag stitch. Take one stitch upwards and outwards across one mesh. Take the second stitch horizontally across one mesh, and bring the third downwards and inwards over one mesh and into the mesh from which you started. Carry the next stitch horizontally across the bottom mesh and repeat in a straight line from the beginning. Miss one line of bars between the rows. The bottom section of this casket shows the simple tambour dot which consists of six stitches worked round a central mesh.

Casket C, 5. Shows a piece of old Limerick tambour taken from a border design. It is worked on a fine diamond-meshed net such as is generally used for the work and shows a characteristic design of small sprays.

CHAPTER IV

CARRICKMACROSS LACE

This lace is of two kinds, Appliqué and Guipure. The first named consists of an appliqué design carried out in muslin and whipped or buttonholed on to net. Needle-run filling stitches are incorporated in selected spaces. The surplus muslin is then cut away close to the cording. Of the two this is the better-wearing lace and the less tedious to work. The Guipure lace has a cut-out design in muslin, the edges of which are whipped over or buttonholed and connected with needle-point bars.

METHOD OF WORKING APPLIQUÉ LACE

The design is prepared on stiff parchment, waxed linen or cambric, as in preparation for Limerick lace. The net is also stretched in the same way, either using a frame or stretching directly over the foundation. In either case the same rules for tacking and fixing should be observed. When these initial stages are complete the muslin is tacked over the net. The three layers must be kept together with meticulous care as any slipping during working will prove fatal to satisfactory results. A very fine sewing needle and the finest cotton should be used to tack the muslin in place, otherwise unsightly stitch-marks will remain when the tackings are removed. As far as possible these threads should run all round the design, following it closely a short distance from the outline, but always leaving this clear. If space allows, a further tacking within the design is advisable· This also should follow the outline, but on the inner side.

The design is now 'corded' or the 'cordonnet' laid. The cord consists of a comparatively thick thread which is couched all round the design with fine close whipping stitches or buttonhole. These should be close enough and tight enough to hold the cord, muslin and net firmly together after the design is cut out. If the stitches are too loose the cord will pull away, leaving frayed edges of muslin.

Great care is needed to keep exactly on the line when working angles and curves. Although the whipping should go through both muslin and net, catching in the parchment must be avoided at all costs. For this reason it is best to trace the design on a shiny surface such as waxed linen. This will turn the point of the needle and blunt it after a time, but it is better to use several needles than run the risk of catching in the foundation.

When the design is thus corded leaf veins and other markings may be added over the appliqué. A thread of the same thickness as the cord is stretched from top to bottom of the vein and overcast with fine thread caught down at several points by taking the stitch right through the muslin. An alternative method is a neat line of back stitch or stem stitch as used in embroidery. All these additions should be made before removing the

66

work from the foundation. When completed, the tacking stitches should be carefully cut at the back and the work gently pulled away from the design. The surplus muslin is now cut away close to the cording. Some people prefer to do this while the work is still on the backing, others find it easier to remove it. In either case the work requires the greatest care and patience in order that no bar may be cut and no rough edge left on the muslin. Special scissors are advisable. These are obtainable from most embroidery shops and are often sold for cut-work. One point is protected with a small thickened end. This should be used on the under or net side of the work. The knob prevents the scissor-points from slipping under a bar and so snipping it together with the muslin.

A variety of filling stitches may be used if desired. Some are common to both Carrickmacross and Limerick laces, others are characteristic of Carrickmacross. If such stitches are to be used they are inserted before the backing is removed, or in the event of this having been done before cutting out the design a small piece of parchment should be tacked under the space to be filled and the net stretched thereon.

There are alternative ways of finishing the edges of this lace. Some workers cut the net and muslin close to the outer cording, others use a machine-made picot edge, while others again employ the third and probably the best method of making a picot on the outer edge while working the cording. This is a very simple operation. As the cording proceeds the thread is twisted into a tiny loop about every eighth of an inch (see Diagram XIII). Two close whipping stitches bind the thread where it crosses and the whipping proceeds to the next loop. Great care is required when cutting out this edging as the picot is on top and therefore liable to catch in the sharp point on the scissors. As there is no net ground to avoid on the under side both net and muslin being cut, it is wiser to reverse the scissors, using the guarded point uppermost. If a buttonhole stitch has been used to appliqué the muslin this makes an excellent edge without further addition.

CARRICKMACROSS GUIPURE

In this lace the design is executed in the same way as in Appliqué, that is, the muslin is stretched over the design and corded as before, but the net ground is omitted. The cording and veining are done exactly as in Appliqué except that there is no underlayer of net to be stitched in.

The filling stitches and ground are worked with needle-point stitches and buttonhole bars of which a good selection is illustrated in Diagrams XVIII to XXX.

Buttonhole bars are often ornamented with 'thorns' as the tiny excrescences are called (Diagram XXIX). The whole piece of work, cording, fillings and ground, should be completed before the muslin is removed from the backing. It is then turned wrong side up and cut out from the back.

Both types of lace require the utmost exactitude and patience and are not very durable when finished, unless

Fig. 7.—Mat in Carrickmacross Guipure

perfectly made. Lovely as they are it is very disheartening to the ardent worker to see the result of her labours falling into rags at the first wash, and this is just what does happen unless the greatest attention and concentration is given to every detail. Therefore the worker who is not prepared to give this care or requires comparatively quick and durable evidence of her industry

69

is not advised to make this lace her first choice. To women who have infinite patience and a passion for detail and fine stitchery I would say proceed, for the work will give you the greatest pleasure and interest, and the results with ordinary care will last for many years.

DESIGNS

There is plenty of scope here for good designs either floral or conventional. Wide expanses of appliqué should be avoided as they will not adhere closely to the net. Small neat floral designs, sprays, well-tied lovers' knots and small conventional designs are the most popular. These usually flow continuously round the edges of the article, thus forming a comparatively strong outer edge of double material, muslin and net, and enabling the worker to cut and finish the edge well. This indicates that a special design is required in the exact shape of the article to be made. Adaptation in this case is not nearly so easy as in Limerick unless the worker has a very good idea of line and drawing. Within the connected border design the net spaces may be as wide as desired. These are often spotted with Limerick dots or filled with needle-run stitches. Designs for Guipure lace should be close and tape-like, leaving no wide spaces for the bars to bridge. As in appliqué, leaves, flowers or other objects should join in such a way that they follow the edges of the desired pattern.

Very excellent results can be obtained by combining the two methods of lace-making on one article. In this

Fig. 8.—A handkerchief square in Carrickmacross Appliqué
and Guipure combined

case the continuous flow of the design should follow the
line dividing the two methods as well as the outer
edges. It pays to give special attention to obtaining a
good design as many of those sold for this lace are
'bitty' and lacking in continuity. These are not only
unattractive when finished but are irritating and
unpleasant to work.

71

MATERIALS

The materials for Carrickmacross as for all other laces should always be of the best. A good firm net with a fine mesh is advisable. The closer the mesh, the more frequently the muslin is stitched to the net during the cording. If a wide mesh is used, several whipping stitches may be taken before a bar is reached, thus making the edges less firm. The muslin should be very fine and firmly woven, otherwise it will pull out easily and fray. This is specially applicable to Guipure lace, as should this fray from the cord there is no means of repairing it. In Appliqué lace a repair can be executed by rewhipping the cord and edge of the muslin back on to the net.

Two thicknesses of thread are required for this work, one for the cord and one for the whipping. The former should be a good crochet cotton, something between a number 50 and a number 80 being suitable for general use. The cotton used for whipping should be fine and strong, numbers 100 to 200 or slightly thicker according to the cord selected. The same fine needles that were used for tacking are also used for the stitchery, although a coarser one may be used for the filling stitches if preferred. These are usually worked in the fine thread used for the whipping, but a slightly thicker one may be used at the worker's discretion.

Diagram XIII shows the method of working Appliqué Carrickmacross. Note the picot edges made with the cord during working.

72

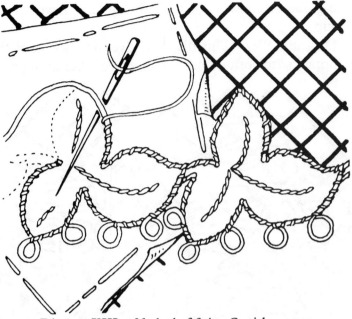

Diagram XIII.—Method of fixing Carrickmacross

NEEDLE-RUN FILLING STITCHES FOR APPLIQUÉ LACE

Many lovely specimens of Carrickmacross Appliqué are finished without the addition of any filling stitches, but if such stitches are to be used a selection can be made from those given in the Limerick needle-run diagrams. A few additional stitches more commonly found in Carrickmacross will be seen in Diagrams XIV, XV and XVI.

Diagram XIV shows a figure eight stitch similar to that in Diagram XI, used in conjunction with a plain looped stitch. These are merely another arrangement of stitches previously illustrated. The two are worked in

73

one group as shown, one mesh being left between each group.

Diagram XV. This diagram gives a variation of the whipped stitch often found in this lace, alternating with

Diagram XIV.—A figure eight stitch

lines of feather stitch. The latter is worked on the mesh exactly the same as an embroidered feather stitch.

Diagram XVI shows the simplest of all the interlaced stitches. It may be worked with a mesh between each row or between groups of two or more rows; alternatively, it can be worked in a solid block without any dividing lines of clear mesh.

74

Diagram XV.—Feather stitch

Diagram XVI.—Simple laced stitch

GUIPURE BARS AND FILLING STITCHES

Diagram XVII shows a typical bar for the Guipure type of lace. These should always be carefully arranged to support the design where the strain is likely to occur. Points of leaves or petals should always be held down and curves well strengthened.

A needle-point bar showing the thorn trimming will be found in Diagram XXIX. Diagrams XXVI and

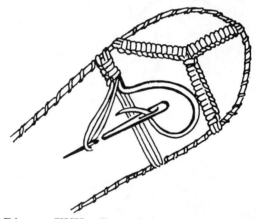

Diagram XVII.—Buttonholed bar for Guipure

XXVII also illustrate stitches commonly found in most needle-point laces including Carrickmacross Guipure.

Diagram XVIII shows a woven leaf vein. The centre vein stitch is woven with a basket stitch and the off-shoot veins left without adornment. This stitch is seen actually worked on the lower leaf of the specimen, D, 1. Two other fillings are shown on this specimen, D, 1, centre leaf; a foundation of loosely worked buttonhole stitch surrounds the space, the stitches being arranged in pairs to come exactly opposite to each other. Some workers strengthen these loops by whipping the heads of the stitches. This is quite optional. The centre is filled by taking two or three large over-stitches between each pair of opposite loops. When one cluster of this stitching is complete, move into the next buttonholed loop with a small whipped stitch. The third leaf fill-

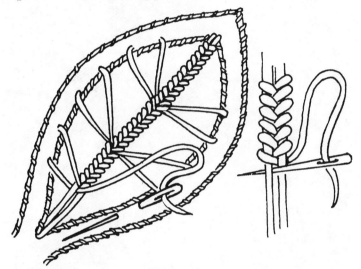

Diagram XVIII.—Woven leaf vein for Guipure

ing in this specimen is also commenced with a row of buttonhole loops, but this time they should not be immediately opposite. The centre of the stitch on the one side should come opposite the joining of the two stitches on the other. The centre space is then filled with a herringbone stitch such as is illustrated in Diagram IV, the buttonholed loops corresponding to the net meshes in the sketch.

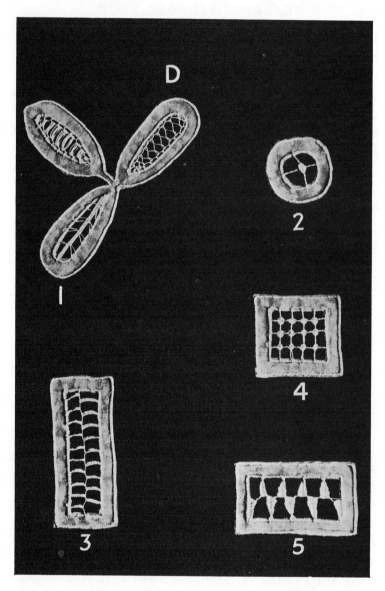

Fig. 9.—Sampler D, Carrickmacross Guipure needle-point fillings

Specimen D, 2, shows the filling of a circle or ring. This may be done in two ways. In the first method the inner line of the circle is corded in the usual way. A thread is then laid from one side of the space to the other, the stitch being taken over the cord. This is then whipped back as far as the centre of the space and from this point another thread is laid at right angles into the cord. Whip this back to the centre and lay the fourth thread in the same way. When the centre is again reached, work a little wheel (see Diagram XXVII) by weaving under and over four or five times at the joining of the threads. Return to the side again by whipping the one remaining single thread.

The alternative method is to work the filling in with the cording thus. Cord half-way round the space. Take the working thread across to the point where the cording commenced and whip it back again. Continue the cording until it is three-quarters of the way round the circle, then take another thread across the space at right angles with the first. Whip this thread only as far as the centre, work the wheel in the same way as before until it is of the required size, and return to the edge by whipping the remaining single thread. Complete the cording and finish neatly.

Specimen D, 3, shows an excellent filling for a long narrow space. It is not nearly so effective if the bars are too long. Commence the work at the centre top of the opening, and take the needle under the cord point downwards into the right-hand edge. Buttonhole from right to left along this thread until about two-thirds are covered. Now take the needle into the left-hand edge and buttonhole from left to right towards the centre. When the thread is two-thirds covered, work back into the right-hand edge, repeating these operations alternately until the space is filled.

Specimen D, 4, illustrates the wheel stitch described in Diagram XXVII. A similarly shaped space can also be filled with the wheel stitch described in Diagram XXVI.

Specimen D, 5, shows the same type of basket stitch as Diagram XXVI, but for the two rows only the thread is laid rather differently. Instead of the triangular arrangement the base thread consists of a twisted stitch like a herringbone. The needle is taken into the cord from the bottom left-hand corner to the top edge, a short distance in. It should pass over the cord and come out at the back on the left of the thread. This crosses the thread for the second stitch, forming a little twist near the cord. Commence to darn the pyramids from a top point and work under and over the two threads until the middle of the space is reached. Whip down the next foundation thread as far as the cord and weave back again towards the centre. Continue in this way until all the points are worked.

One other method of filling, not illustrated here, is often found in Carrickmacross lace. It consists of a foundation of buttonhole stitches worked over the cording as in the centre leaf filling of Specimen D, 1. The buttonhole heads are then whipped and the thread tightened so that it is taut and firm at the edge. On this base is worked a spoke and wheel design as Specimen D, 2. More spokes can be added if a large circle is to be filled.

CHAPTER V

IRISH CROCHET

IRISH CROCHET or Irish Crochet Lace, as it is usually called, is not in reality lace, though it is one of the loveliest products of the Emerald Isle. In method it closely follows the principles of our modern crochet, employing most of the common stitches known to us all. In design and general appearance the work does closely resemble a very dainty lace. This is not surprising as it was first made in imitation of one of the Spanish laces. It is perhaps rather straying from our appointed path to include this work in these pages, but there are such possibilities here awaiting the adaptation of the modern needle-woman that it seems a pity to exclude it from the list.

To give detailed instructions would be far too lengthy and complicated, so the general principles only will be outlined and the worker left to follow her individual inclinations. Although the methods are the same as those followed in ordinary crochet the designs and finished effects are as far removed from the modern stereotyped mechanical patterns as hand-made net is from a common dish-cloth. The lace is built up from a series of sprays or shapes, floral or conventional, crocheted in the finest thread with a tiny hook. These are ultimately tacked to a suitable stiff background bearing the design and are joined with crochet bars and needle-point or crochet fillings.

The sprays are all worked over a cord or padding consisting of several strands of thread. This gives the firmness and shape needed to gain satisfactory results. As no two workers shape the cord in the same way so the design never works out quite identical in different hands. The same observation is true regarding the ground-work and bars, for no two workers will set these at the same angle or execute the filling stitches in the same way. Thus it will readily be seen the work lends itself to an infinite variety of interpretations and the worker who loves to create her own designs will find it an ever-abiding source of interest.

DESIGNS

Although the ultimate layout of the motifs and the completion of the design can be left to the individual, some definite plan of campaign should be prearranged, as assembling the work effectively takes considerable practice. The simplest course for a beginner is to purchase a ready-planned foundation together with instructions for making the necessary motifs. When familiar with the work the more interesting way is to plan out the design for oneself. This is really considerably simpler than it appears. First it is as well to ascertain what constitutes a good or bad design. Lumpy effects are to be avoided at all costs. Nothing looks less lace-like and less attractive than one or two massive sprays joined up with a maze of meaningless bars. Avoid, too, a series of tiny isolated sprays joined up in like manner. The best designs are composed of neat, close, well-proportioned motifs, practically touching, and having the intermediate spaces bridged and filled with stitches and bars which have some relation to the design as a whole.

When planning a given article such as a collar or cuffs, first cut the exact pattern in waxed linen or stiff cambric, excluding from the size the space to be occupied by the lace edging, as this is worked beyond the foundation after the motifs have been joined. Next work up a few sprays and arrange them artistically on the pattern. When a general scheme has been decided upon, trace in roughly the different sprays in their allotted places. It will then be seen how many of each kind are required to complete the article, also the best-shaped motifs to fill certain angles and spaces.

MATERIALS

An ordinary crochet hook may be used provided it is very fine, but a special Irish Crochet hook is recommended. This has a much shorter shaft and a dumpy fat handle. For such fine stitches and threads it is easier and quicker to handle and control. A few small round meshes are required in various sizes for shaping the cord rings which form the base of many designs. If such meshes are not handy some pencils or knitting-pins of different thicknesses may be used as a substitute. A cotton thread is generally used, either a strong fine crochet cotton or a specially made lace thread obtainable in various sizes, number 80 being suitable for fine lace, and number 36 for coarse. There are many intermediate sizes in both cottons. The padding thread should be considerably thicker than the working thread. A suitable cotton is procurable in skeins. All these threads are made in the usual lace shades, white, cream, écru and black.

At one time coloured silks were much used for the work, especially when it was used for dress decorations. This fashion has died out somewhat in recent years. If, however, the worker does favour this medium it can be obtained in balls or skeins of suitable thickness.

Before starting work it is advisable to obtain a small box or a few envelopes in which to keep the finished sprays, otherwise they have a habit of disappearing just when wanted.

A few typical specimen motifs have been worked out in a thick thread and the instructions given. Only very simple motifs have been designed to illustrate the different ways of forming circles, petals and leaves. These should enable the worker to become acquainted with the craft. When it has been mastered she will find it quite easy to combine and extend these methods in the making of larger and more elaborate sprays.

When commencing a spray, start with an ample length of cord as too many joins make the work bulky and uneven. If a join must be made, lap the new length over the old and crochet over both for a short distance. As each petal or small section of the motif is completed the cord should be drawn up slightly and the work neatly pressed into shape between finger and thumb. On this shaping depends much of the success of the finished article. The crochet covering the cord should be firm and even and rather tight.

Specimen E, 1. This little group shows rings of different sizes. These usually form the base of flowers and leaves or the centres of conventional motifs. If a space occurs in the ground too large to be bridged by bars, rings may be placed in the space and the bars radiated from them to the design. Tiny rings may be arranged in groups to form berries or bunches of grapes. They may also be used in circles round larger rings to form attractive motifs. Their shape can be pulled into an oval and held thus with needle-point fillings. To make a ring take a mesh or round object such as a pencil and wind the cord round it ten or fifteen times. Remove this with great care and work double crochet into the ring so formed until the cord is well covered. If the design is to be extended the number of double crochets worked into the ring should be arranged accordingly (see Specimen E, 2). Extensions may be made by working a row of looped chain or treble crochet with chain between round the ring, the cord being joined in again when the petals are commenced.

Specimen E, 2. *A small rose.* Wind a length of cord ten times round a number 4 knitting-pin. Slip it off carefully and work twenty-four double crochets into the ring. To complete the circle join the first stitch to the last with a single crochet. A little care is required to hold the cord in place until the first few stitches are worked. After a little practice this becomes quite easy.

85

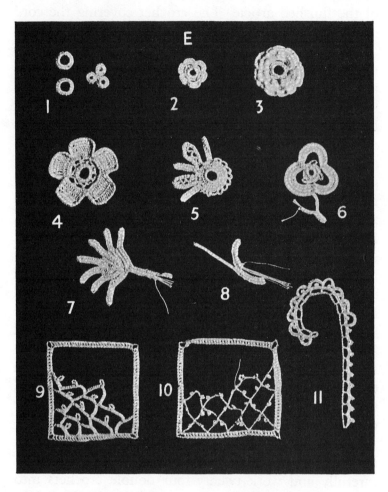

Fig. 10.—Sampler E, specimens of Irish Crochet

To form the petals work over two strands of cord. Join this to the ring by making a loop in the middle of the thread and working a single crochet over the loop into the last stitch. (When four or six strands of cord are required take two or three lengths and double them over, joining in the same way.) Now make nine treble crochets over the cord only. Miss three stitches on the ring and work a double crochet into the fourth, taking this stitch over the cord, thus attaching it to the ring. Tighten the cord until the petal is nicely curved, then form another in the same way until six are arranged at even distances round the ring. Join the last petal to the base of the first with a single crochet and finish at the back by tying the cord and the working thread together as inconspicuously as possible.

Specimen E, 3. *A large rose.* This is commenced in the same way as the small rose but with a slightly larger ring into which twenty-eight double crochets are worked. On this base work seven petals, each composed of nine treble crochet. The second row of petals is worked in the same way. Continuing on the cord work twelve treble crochet for each, catching each petal down with a double crochet where those of the preceding row meet. Any number of rows may be added in this manner, but the number of stitches used for each petal should be increased by two in each new row.

Specimen E, 4. This flower shows another type of petal which can be varied in many ways by altering the filling within the petals or changing the design of the centre ring.

Make a ring on an average-sized lead pencil and

87

work into it twenty-seven double crochets. For the second round work five chain, miss two stitches on the ring, and double crochet into the third. Complete the circle in this way. Work another round in the same stitch, taking the double crochets into the centre stitches of the chains.

Join in four strands of cord and work in double crochet over chain and cord, taking five stitches into each loop. Leave the cord and work nine treble crochet into the next nine stitches on the ring. Turn the work with three chain and work another row double crochet. Turn again with three chain and work a third row. This constitutes the filling for one petal. The block of stitches so formed can be worked in other ways to vary the appearance of the flower. For example, chain loops can be used in the place of treble crochet, or the treble crochet may be reduced toward the tip, making the petal pointed. The only thing to bear in mind is to work an uneven number of rows in order to bring the working thread on to the opposite side of the petal from where it started. Do not break the thread, lay it flat down the side of the petal and catch it with a single crochet at the base. It can then be worked in with the cord later. This brings the working thread to the correct place to start the second petal. Work this exactly like the first and repeat the operation until there are five petals at equal distances round the centre. The working thread has now reached the point where the cord was left. Pick this up again and work round each petal with double crochet, taking the stitches over the cord into the edges.

This method of building up petals can be applied to leaves. Alternatively the number of petals can be altered; thus three would make a shamrock. The number of stitches round the ring must divide equally into the number of petals required. This can be arranged when making the ring.

Specimen E, 5. The thistle-shaped flower shows two more petal arrangements. The narrow solid ones are composed of a row of double crochet worked over the cord to the required length. At the top of the petal turn the cord over and work back into the first row, catching it to the ring at the base with a single crochet. The open-worked petal is commenced in the same way, but the cord is left at the top and two rows of chain loops worked down and back again, bringing the thread to the cord once more. The cord is then picked up and the second edge worked like the first. These two arrangements may be used as shown or worked all round the ring to form a circular flower. Each type of petal may if desired be used singly, for either flowers or leaves. For any thistle-shaped flower the bottom part of the ring should be slightly enlarged and ornamented with a few extra rows of stitches. The cord for this can be carried round from the base of the last petal worked.

Specimen E, 6. Leaves can be built up in several ways. The little shamrock in the specimen is made rather on the lines of the rose, three petals only being used. Here are the exact instructions which can be varied in size if required.

Make a ring of the cord by winding it ten times on

a number 4 knitting pin and working twenty double crochet into the ring. Work round again in double crochet. Now work four double crochet, six chain to form a picot, six more double crochet, six chain; repeat until the ring is filled, finishing with four double crochet. Join in four strands of cord and work twenty-five treble crochet over the cord alone; work one double crochet and a single crochet into the ring between the first and second picot loops. Tighten the cord to a nice curve and work the second and third leaflets in the same way. Continuing the cord, work a second row exactly over the first. The specimen shows the cord continued to form a stem, the bottom part being worked double and made to branch out ready for the next leaf. A spray of three or four shamrocks makes a very attractive unit.

Specimen E, 7. This specimen shows another form of leaf. It is built up on a long length of cord. About four strands would give adequate padding. Work twenty double crochet to form the bottom of the stem. Continue twenty more of the same stitches and turn the cord, missing one stitch and working back over nineteen. Turn the cord again and work ten stitches joined to the last block and ten over the cord only. Repeat these rows until there are four points. The last of these forms the tip of the leaf and may be longer if desired. Continue to work down the other side of the leaf joining the base of each point to its opposite number with a single crochet. When the stem is reached, continue over the cord for the required length.

A good fern leaf can be made by adding more points and drawing up the under cord of each to give it a nice curve. In this case the points will only be joined up for the first two or three stitches instead of half-way.

Specimen E, 8. Here is shown the construction of stems. They are worked over cords usually rather thicker than those used for flowers and leaves. They may consist of any number of rows to give the required thickness and branch stems may be formed at any point by working on the cord or a few strands of the cord only. Where possible the stem cord should be continued from the base of a flower or leaf to save a join. If this is not possible the stem should be attached as neatly as possible at the back of the work. When the requisite number of sprays are made they are tacked in place on the foundation and joined with crochet bars. The foundation, as previously stated, is cut to the exact size of the pattern excluding the border which is worked beyond the foundation. The motifs may be arranged touching the edge of the parchment and the ground should be worked in such a way as to form an even line round the pattern on which to work the border. A little care is required to place the bars at suitable angles. This is largely a matter of practice. When working the ground on the foundation the latter should be folded sharply across at the place of working in order to give the crochet hook free play. The crease must be altered frequently as the work proceeds and the parchment should be spread out occasionally to ascertain if the ground is lying flat and not dragging the design at any point.

Specimen E, 9. *Bars.* A firm bar is worked by making a chain from one point to another and then working back over it with double crochet. A picot is made about the centre of each loop by working half-way in double crochet, then making eight chain and catching the last into the first with a single crochet, from thence continuing in double crochet to the end of the bar. It cannot be stressed too often that these bars need careful arrangement to support the design wherever necessary. They should never be too long and straggling. Nine or ten chain make a good average length bar.

Specimen E, 10. A lighter bar can be made by working the chain stitch only with little picot trimmings. This makes a dainty ground but is rather apt to stretch and pull out of shape more than the first method. A complete picot bar consists of nine chain and one single crochet into the fifth stitch from the needle, nine more chain and a single crochet into the fifth from the needle and four chain. Starting along one side of a space work a bar and stretch it along the space marking the point midway between the two picots. Make a single crochet attaching the end of the bar at this point, so forming a loop. Work a series of these along the side of the space to be filled. Creep up the side with single crocheting and return across the space with like bars, attaching the ends of the second row between the picots of the first.

Specimen E, 11. The design is now joined up and ready for a neatening edge. If the base on which this is to be worked does not appear to be sufficiently

Fig. 11.—Some small Irish Crochet motifs, joined and edged

connected and solid, a row of chain may be worked round the whole foundation and joined to the design with a single crochet wherever it touches. If the design has been well planned and the bars well thought out this should not be necessary.

Edgings for Irish Crochet can be of any depth, and as simple or complicated as the worker desires. The specimen, E, 11, shows the simplest of all borders, but on the same principle something more elaborate and decorative can be built.

Working along the chain or edge of the ground make a treble crochet into every fourth stitch. If the edge is curved, work four chain between each of these stitches. If straight, work three. Into the loops thus formed work three double crochet over the chain, then make a picot of four chain and work three more double crochet. Repeat this in the next space and so on round the whole edge. This pattern is sufficient for a narrow border, but it may be increased as indicated on the upper curve of the specimen by working loops of eight chain and catching them down between the picots of the last row. The work is then turned over and each chain loop filled with double crochet. Such loops can be increased or built upon each other for any depth or in varied sizes with or without picots.

CHAPTER VI

RETICELLA WORK

RETICELLA is one of the earliest forms of lace-making. It embodies the principles of all needle-point laces and is a direct descendant of the old cut-work and 'punto in aria'. It is a lace that should particularly commend itself to the beginner as it is comparatively coarse and easy to handle. The designs, being geometrical, combine perfectly with modern furnishings and are therefore a delightful way of making attractive motifs for house-linen. Made in very thick thread it would prove charming for trimming curtains and bedspreads. Although this is a coarse lace of geometrical design the same principles apply to all the lovely flowered designs of the finer needle-point laces.

On studying the diagrams illustrating Reticella stitches the worker may be surprised to see that the needle is apparently pointing in the wrong direction, giving a clumsy appearance to the method of working. This is the Italian style and has much in its favour. The usual method of working with the needle towards the body as in ordinary needlework is quite permissible and is taught by most schools in this country.

The Italian principle is not nearly so difficult to learn as it appears at first, the advantage being that the work is built from the bottom upwards, so that the finished

95

Fig. 12.—Finished Reticella on a linen ground

section is naturally held between the finger and thumb of the left hand during working. This without further trouble flattens and presses the lace into a good shape. It also prevents too much pull on the first row of stitches during the working of the subsequent rows, the completed stitches being protected by the pressure of the fingers which is naturally increased when there is any added strain such as a knotted thread pulling against it. Another point in favour of this method is the increased light one gets from working beyond the shadow of the hand. It is an important consideration when working the finer types of needle-point.

METHODS OF WORKING

The foundation thread or Fil de Trace as it is called is couched on a stiff backing or parchment bearing the design. The couching of this thread is very important as on it depends the whole success of the work. A coarse thread is required for the Fil de Trace, but the finest sewing cotton is used for the couching, the stitches of which must be taken perfectly straight across the outlining thread.

If these couching stitches are slanted in any way they will interfere with the needle-point stitches when the time comes to work them. Another very important point is to keep the Fil de Trace perfectly even over the line of the design, as a wavy outline will cause wavy uneven lace. In order to assist smooth laying of the foundation thread it must be untwisted from time to time and made pliant between the fingers. Unnecessary joins should be avoided, as this is apt to weaken the lace and cause unevenness in the outline. Should a join be unavoidable the old and new lengths are overlapped for a short distance and the double thickness couched as before.

A good worker will start with a sufficient length of couching thread to complete a motif. It should be of double thread worked in the following manner. The thread is looped in the middle and the first couching stitch taken through the loop. The first length of outlining is couched over the double thread. Assuming one is outlining the specimen (see Sampler F, I), take the foundation threads from corner to corner across the centre of the motif. Turn the corner carefully and work on to the first intersecting line. Now take a single strand of the Fil de Trace and couch it to the end of the branch line and back to where it joins the second thread. Continue over both strands until the next branch line is reached, then proceed as before, always using the longer of the two ends. Where secondary lines branch out from any lines being couched with a single thread, these should be worked at the same time, the strand being couched up and back over the same line, joining in again at the point from which it branched. Work the lines on the right with the outgoing thread, and those on the left when returning.

Particular attention is required to see the best way of joining in the circles. In the case of the specimen design, the larger one is couched once, the thread branching from a crossing spoke. The thread then travels down another small portion of the spoke to the smaller circle, and from thence completes the spoke. The return journey is made over the same lines, the final row of the larger circle eventually joining the second thread to complete the outline.

Special consideration should be given to the layout of any design, to see the best way in which to preserve the continuity of the Fil de Trace. Where two couching threads cross they should be interlocked to add strength to the structure. Some of the smaller bars of the design are added during the working of the needle-point stitches.

The Fil de Trace is now worked upon and the design built up. A ring may be buttonholed and graduated points of buttonholing worked thereon, each succeeding row being worked into the heads of the last. Bars may be added where required for support. These should be whipped or buttonholed. If the bar is to be built up into part of the design, and is required as a base for other stitches, it should be buttonholed. Buttonhole bars may be ornamented with thorns and picots.

Attractive edges may be built up from a series of cord loops buttonholed over and ornamented with picots.

The primary stitches used throughout Reticella are buttonholing, whipping and weaving or basket stitch, but the work, having been handed down for so many centuries, has appeared in different forms and under different names all over the world, each class of work using slightly different fillings. It is now almost inseparably mixed with drawn fabric work, and the stitches used are found in many kinds of lace and drawn thread embroidery. Although in true Reticella only the simplest stitches appear (see Diagrams XIX to XXIV), it would be foolish to lay down any fixed rules for the filling, as the worker may find a lovely and more elaborate conception which has greater appeal. The pyramids (Diagram XXVI) are often used. The most usual form of wheel is a small buttonholed circle worked on a laid outline round whipped spokes. The photographic illustration shows this particularly clearly. Another attractive wheel is shown in Diagram XXVII.

In more complicated types of needle-point whole grounds are filled in with a loose mesh like buttonhole stitch upon which other stitches are worked. Space does not permit of a detailed account of all the different ways of working buttonholing. It must suffice to say that the variations are almost innumerable, ranging from the closest tightly worked rows to the daintiest cobweb fine openwork.

An alternative foundation can be made by drawing sufficient threads from a length of evenly woven linen. This gives an excellent firm base and prevents the necessity for inserting the motifs after working. If such a foundation is used the bars of thread should first be worked over in basket stitch to make them solid (Diagram XXI). They are then worked upon as before, any circles or small crossing lines being added to the structure.

Specimen F, 1, shows the simplest of geometrical designs with the foundation threads laid and the filling partly worked.

Specimen F, 2 shows the preparation of a drawn fabric ground for this same work.

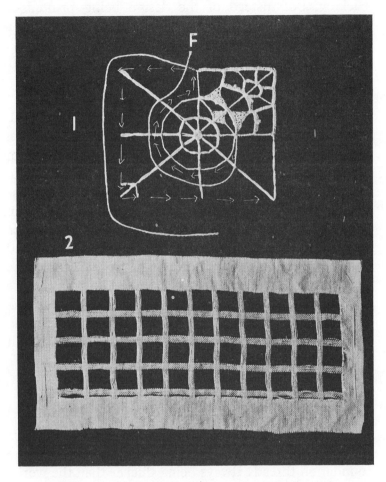

Fig. 13.—Sampler F, foundations for Reticella work

In this method the linen is usually tacked over a firm backing, but instead of the design being printed or stamped thereon it is either copied from a drawing or a piece of already completed work.

DESIGNS

These are in the case of Reticella always geometrical. With a little practice the worker can progress from simple beginnings to more elaborate arrangements of her own patterning. This is the most interesting way to work. Should, however, the worker be lacking in ideas she can purchase ready-stamped foundations upon which to lay her foundation threads. Even so she will be tempted to vary the filling stitches from time to time and so change the whole aspect of the work. Should she be interested in the finer types of needle-point, more specialized knowledge will be required. Although the methods are identical, points of difficulty are likely to arise in outlining intricate designs and filling in spacious backgrounds.

MATERIALS

Almost any thread can be used for this work. For lace motifs a well-twisted crochet cotton is suitable, the foundation threads always being thicker than the working threads. The couching is done with the finest sewing cotton. Other suitable materials are smooth flax lace threads, lightly twisted single strand embroidery cottons and many of the finer knitting silks. In addition to threads the worker will require a good selection of sewing needles of various sizes, a pair of small sharp embroidery scissors, and a suitable foundation upon which to lay the threads.

DIAGRAMS

In copying these stitches the worker is reminded that the needle may be reversed and the stitch worked inwards towards the body in the usual way. As this is the simplest method and the most natural to adopt the

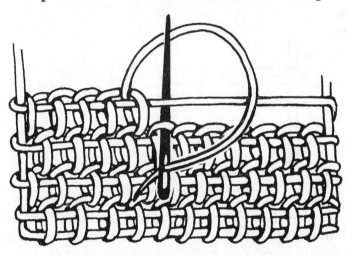

Diagram XIX.—Close buttonhole filling

more complicated style has been selected for illustration, its advantages having been previously outlined.

Diagram XIX. Here is shown a square space filled with a close buttonhole stitch. The first guide line is laid close to the outline of the space and the stitch is worked over the two rows. From the finishing point of the first row the thread is whipped up the side of the space to the depth of one stitch and there knotted once round the foundation thread. From here a second guide line is stretched to the opposite side and buttonholed back, the stitches going over the line into the heads of those of the first row. This buttonholing may be worked as openly or as closely as desired.

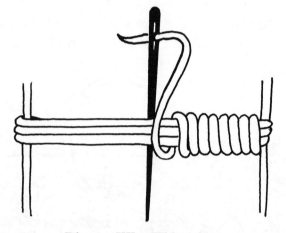

Diagram XX.—Whipped bar

Diagram XX. This illustrates a whipped bar. The whipping may bind any number of threads according to the thickness and strength of the bar required.

Diagram XXI. This basket-worked bar is very simple and though it is much used in Reticella is common to many other laces and embroideries.

Diagram XXII illustrates a buttonhole edging which is worked over a cord. Similar loops can be built up to form fancy edgings such as appear in the photograph.

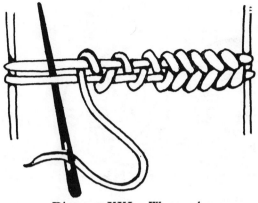

Diagram XXI.—Woven bar

Diagram XXIII. Shows clearly a method of working an open buttonhole stitch held in place by binding

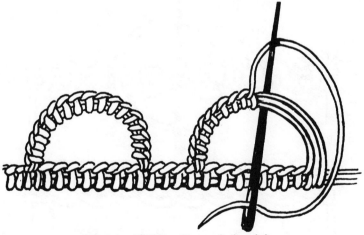

Diagram XXII.—Buttonhole edging

the heads of each pair of stitches with a third worked across the top.

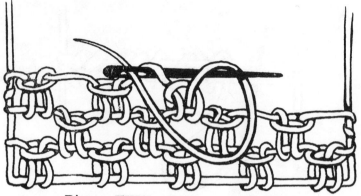

Diagram XXIII.—Open buttonhole filling

Diagram XXIV. This drawing indicates how a double-sided buttonholed bar is worked.

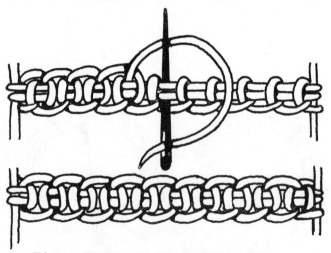

Diagram XXIV.—Double-sided buttonhole bars

For the more complicated needle-point stitches used in the finer point laces refer to Diagrams XXV to XXX

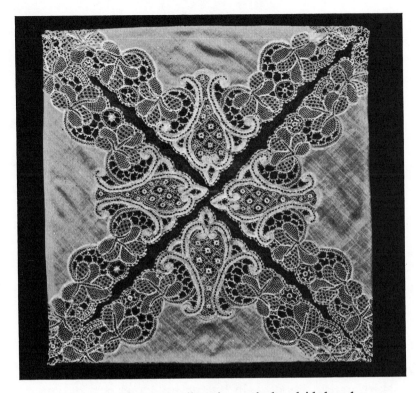

Fig. 14.—Modern needle-point worked on laid threads

and Sampler H in the Devonshire Point section, where a selection of these is illustrated and fully explained.

The method of laying threads and working over the cord so formed applies to all such point laces as Irish Point (Youghal) and Rose Point, etc., as distinct from the Honiton and Braid Point group, although the same stitches are used in all.

CHAPTER VII

PRINCESS LACE

Princess lace is a delightful and comparatively modern combination of methods which produce an exceedingly dainty lace suitable for personal wear or the daintier more luxurious articles of house-linen, such as best table mats, or cheval sets and tray-cloths for use under glass.

It is particularly to be recommended to the beginner because it is exceedingly simple to make and yet provides the opportunity for practising some of the more difficult lace methods in a simplified form. For instance, the arranging of the braid design on the comparative firmness of the net provides excellent practice for the more intricate tacking of the braid needed for Devonshire point. Then again by the judicious cutting away of leaf and flower centres needle-point stitches of the simpler kind may be introduced, while the caskets formed with the braided outline provide excellent spaces to try out new combinations of needle-run stitches.

METHOD

The ground for this lace is a machine-made net usually of a strong octagonal mesh. This is tacked

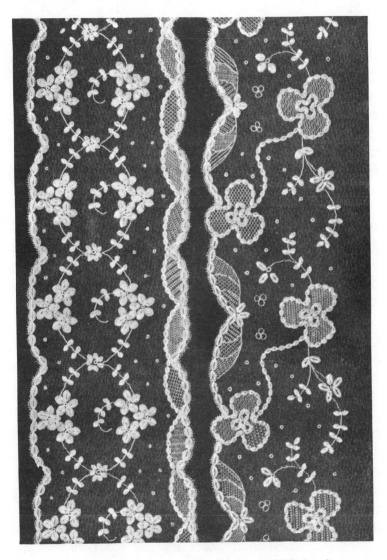

Fig. 15.—Princess lace showing borders of filled caskets

smoothly over the foundation bearing the design. It may be stretched with or without a frame, the rules relating to Limerick needle-run being applicable.

The greater part of the design is then appliquéd with small lengths of machine-made braid, such as are shown in the illustration. The remainder of the design is completed with needle-run or in some cases needle-point stitches; for these instructions refer to the Diagrams and Samplers on needle-point and needle-run laces.

The outstanding units of the designs such as leaflets, flower petals, edges and borders are all formed of Honiton braids of varied shapes. It is most interesting to notice how different are the effects gained by using different braids. These should only be cut where absolutely necessary. The borders should be continuous where possible, and in the case of flower petals two can usually be made with one length of braid if folded towards the centre. Where it is necessary to cut the braid it should be bound with a few twists of thread and the ends tucked neatly under and caught down with the whipping. When the correct braid has been selected and cut it is arranged over the design and tacked into place, then overstitched (whipped) neatly all round the edges. The shaped Honiton braids lend themselves easily to the curves and twists of the design, but some of the straight point braids require more careful handling. The outer edges should be arranged first, then if necessary the inner edges can be finely whipped apart from the net and drawn up to the required curve, the drawn edge being whipped

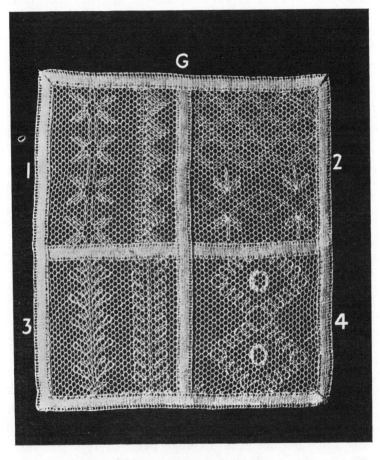

Fig. 16.—Sampler G, arrangements of simple darning used in
Princess lace

again, this time on to the net. The thread used for whipping should in no case be too tightly drawn, as this will spoil the appearance of the finished work. Finer stems than can be made with braid may be darned in the same way as a needle-run outline.

The design is now filled in as fully or as slightly as desired, using fancy darning or needle-run stitches. A few variations of the former appear in Sampler G. These are so simple that they may be followed from the photograph without further explanation.

All filling stitches should start well up to the braid. If the worker finds it easier, the bordering edge concerned may be whipped after the stitches are worked.

DESIGNS

Small graceful floral designs are the most effective. These can usually be found amongst the lighter lace designs or those prepared for Broderie Anglaise or braiding.

MATERIALS

A good net ground such as suggested for Limerick and Carrickmacross laces is suitable. A selection of braids such as those illustrated may be purchased from any Lace School at an average price of $1\frac{1}{2}d$. per yard. The worker will also need a suitable cotton or flax thread for the filling stitches, a very fine sewing cotton for the whipping, a good selection of sewing needles suitable for these threads and some sharp embroidery scissors.

The stock designs are ready printed on strong foundations, but should the worker design her own lace the necessary length of waxed linen must be obtained.

The edge of the lace usually forms part of the design. This is therefore braided and the surplus net cut close at the back. Care should be taken when tacking threads are removed to see that none of the work is pulled. Made in a good net with close braid carefully whipped the lace will wash and wear for many years, even if given quite hard use.

CHAPTER VIII

MODERN NEEDLE-POINT LACES
(BRAID POINT)

WITHIN this large group lie modern Flemish, modern Venetian Point, English or Devonshire Point, Renaissance and in fact all the machine-aided replicas of some of the older point laces, many of which have several names varying in the country or district in which they are made. Some people include Princess, otherwise known as Duchess, lace in this category, but as net is used in the ground and needle-run stitches introduced in the fillings this cannot be classed as true point. These modern laces are based on excellent reproductions of Honiton, Battenberg, Bruges, Russian, Flemish and other braids.

The filling stitches are those used throughout the ages in needle-point laces. The number of these must be countless as generations of lace-makers have arranged and rearranged them, each seeking some individual touch wherewith to seal her handiwork.

Of all modern needle-craft point laces perhaps give the greatest scope for individuality, the same design becoming totally different when carried out with different braids or an alternative grouping of the fillings. For this reason no rules can be laid down. The worker must be free to follow her own inclinations.

Fig. 17.—Braid Point, known as English Point, utilizing many of the stitches shown on sampler H

It will suffice to say that taste and judgment should be exercised to array the filling stitches in such a way as to add strength and durability at the required points without losing the fairy-like fragility which is characteristic of the best specimens of this work.

The method followed is to tack the requisite lengths of braid on to a stiff foundation bearing the design and afterwards filling the spaces with needle-point stitches. The tacking should be made down the centre of the braid or, in the case of a very narrow one, a wide herringbone may cross it from side to side, thus avoiding any unnecessary strain on the threads. The outer lines of curves and corners should be fixed first. Then, if necessary, corners can be mitred and curves whipped and drawn into place.

The mitring of corners and any joins in the braid should be done on the wrong side, and afterwards pressed and tacked into the correct position. Such joins should only be made when absolutely unavoidable.

When the design is fixed the filling stitches should be carefully thought out and worked in accordance with a preconceived plan.

DESIGNS

The designs for this work are so numerous and can look so totally different worked up in individual ways that it seems unnecessary to go to the trouble of preparing anything original. A really good design ready stamped on a firm ground costs very little and can be used over and over again.

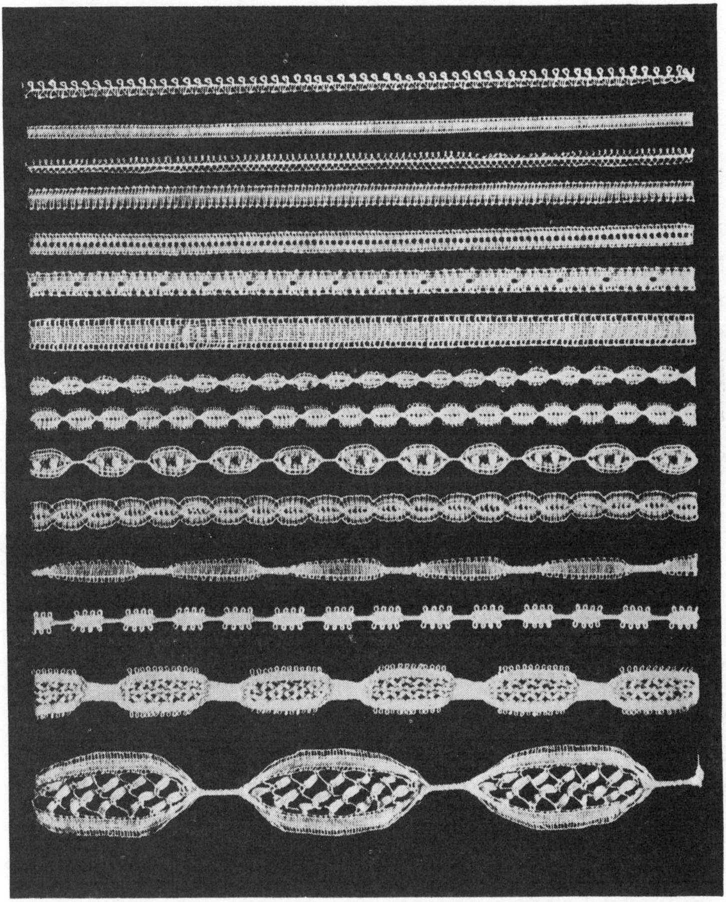

Fig. 18.—Some specimen braids and gimp edgings used in
Princess lace and Braid Point

MATERIALS

A selection of the necessary braids, only a few of which are illustrated, can be obtained from any good needlework department. From these the worker can make her choice. It is also possible to purchase linen thread rings of various sizes which may be inserted here and there to reduce large spaces where filling stitches are used. A better method is to make these rings on a mesh, working over a cord as in Irish Crochet but substituting a buttonhole stitch for the double crochet. It is then possible to work the ring with the same thread as the filling stitches which gives the lace a much better and more professional appearance. It is not usual to introduce rings in very fine specimens of lace.

A linen thread is recommended for all fillings. The thickness should, of course, depend upon the texture of the braid selected. Quite good results can be gained by using a fine thread for filling leaves, flowers, or centres of units and a thicker one for the ground.

An assortment of fine needles and some sharp-pointed scissors complete the necessary equipment.

FILLING STITCHES

It is not possible to describe all the variations of filling stitches, even if one could hope to make a complete collection of them. Most of them are, however, evolved from a few basic stitches, which are clearly illustrated in the diagrams.

Diagram XXV shows a net-like arrangement of buttonhole stitch, by far the most popular basic stitch of the whole group.

Diagram XXVI. This illustrates a typical pyramid stitch which taken in conjunction with Diagram XXI and Specimen D, 5, forms the foundation of quite a number of needle-point fillings.

Diagram XXVII. This shows a wheel common to all needle-point laces, varying only in size and the number and position of the spokes on which the circles are darned. Note that spokes may be closely whipped (see Diagram XX), buttonholed (see Diagram XVI), or simply twisted as in Diagram XXVII and Specimen D, 2.

Diagram XXVIII gives a simple knotted arrangement for veining, and may be enlarged upon and strengthened by working the threads over with basket stitch (see Diagram XVIII).

Diagram XXIX shows a buttonhole bar ornamented with the traditional 'thorn'. This is made by pulling out the head of a stitch at intervals along the bar. The extended loop is fixed to the foundation with a pin until five or six buttonhole stitches have been worked over it. The needle is then taken back to the bar by running it down through the centre of the thorn. After working the first stitch round the extended loop some people carry the working thread up to the pin and work backwards towards the bar. In this case the first stitch taken against the pin should go into the loop and be pulled up tightly; the remainder are worked over the two threads as before.

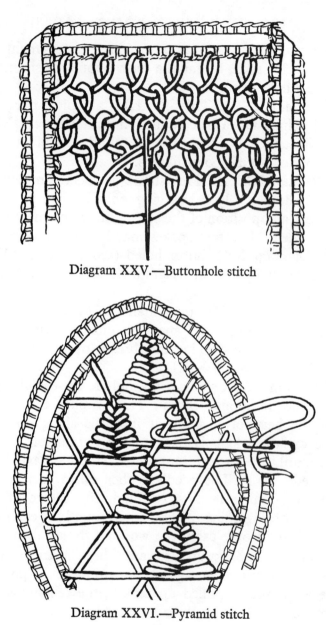

Diagram XXV.—Buttonhole stitch

Diagram XXVI.—Pyramid stitch

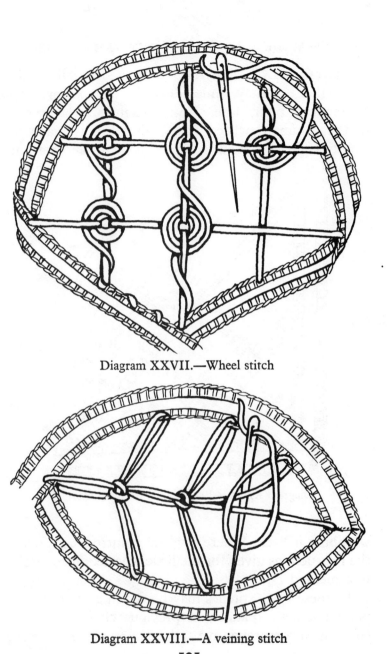

Diagram XXVII.—Wheel stitch

Diagram XXVIII.—A veining stitch

Diagram XXX illustrates a twisted stitch of the herringbone variety, much used in the coarser types of modern point lace. It is merely an elaboration of the common twisted bar. This latter is made by simply laying a thread from one point to another and

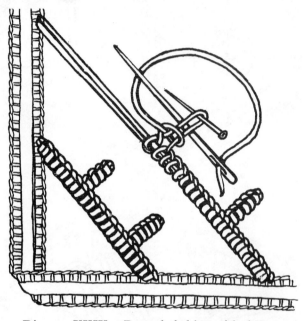

Diagram XXIX.—Buttonholed bar with thorn

whipping it back. Where a wheel is introduced follow the instructions given for the little wheeled filled circle, first method D, 2.

To these basic stitches may be added all the needle-point stitches explained in previous chapters. These comprise a comprehensive collection on which to work.

Illustrations of how they may be varied appear in the Samplers.

Specimen H, 1. *Point de Venise.* This is a very useful form of buttonholing that can be used for both edges and fillings. It is composed of a large loose loop into which several small tight stitches are worked. The small stitches commence in the centre of each large

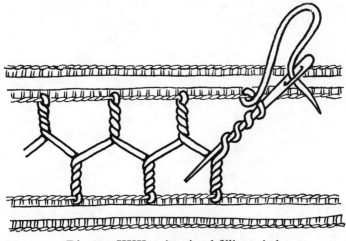

Diagram XXX.—A twisted filling stitch

loop and are worked back to where the looped stitch finishes. That is to say, the small stitches are worked over both loop and working thread. The return row, if used for a ground, is a large single buttonholed loop.

Specimen H, 2. *A useful ground-work.* For this stitch the foundation rows are first laid at even distances across the space. The second row is laced with a zig-zag stitch between the edge and the first foundation

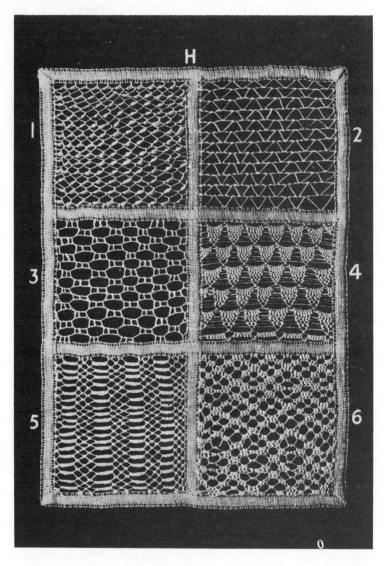

Fig. 19.—Sampler H, showing a variety of needle-point stitches

row, and the third row is whipped back on the foundation thread, every third stitch catching down a point of the preceding row. Work these last two rows alternately until the foundation lines are covered.

Specimen H, 3. Point d'Espagne. This stitch is worked from left to right. Insert the needle in the edge of the braid, keeping the thread turned to the right, bring it out inside the loop formed by the thread, passing the needle from the back of the loop through it. Pass the needle under the stitch and bring it out in front, thus twisting the thread twice. At the end of the row attach the head of the stitch to the braid and return, taking one over stitch into each hole, thus returning to the right-hand side in readiness for the second row of stitching. Variations of this stitch may be made by working in groups of two, three or four twists.

Specimen H, 4. Fan Stitch. Here again is simply an arrangement of buttonholing. Work the first row in wide loose loops. Into each, working from right to left, make eight (or an even number) of close buttonhole stitches. Return, working into the heads of these stitches, thus making one less stitch in each succeeding row. This lengthens the joining stitches. Continue working until one stitch only is worked into the point of the pyramid. This forms a second row of wide loops on which to work the next pattern.

Specimen H, 5. Flemish Lace Stitch. For the first row, work into the border two close buttonhole stitches, a short loop, two more close buttonhole stitches, and a long loop. Work thus to the end of the row. Return, working seven close buttonhole stitches into each long loop, and two into the short loop. Repeat these rows alternately until the space is full.

Specimen H, 6. Genoa Lace Stitch. This shows a lacy pattern obtained by slightly rearranging the loops and close buttonholing of the two foregoing stitches.

CHAPTER IX

FILET LACE

F<small>ILET</small> or Lacis, as it is sometimes called, is a delightful hard-wearing lace, particularly suitable for practical purposes. As in Reticella the neat compact rather formal lines of the designs combine perfectly with modern fashions and furnishings.

For true filet the foundation net is hand-made with a netting needle, although the same system of darning the design may be applied on a square machine-made mesh. To work the design the made net is stretched in a carefully wrapped metal frame of exactly the right size to hold the work, and the design is worked in by means of darning stitch. This is commenced from the left-hand bottom corner of the design, going under and over every mesh. When the end of the design is reached, make the return journey to the starting-point. Now cross-darn the net to the point where the design decreases or increases, then darn again from left to right. Thus the design is being completed from the left, the unfinished horizontal rows protruding on the right. When a section of the design is finished, it is 'edged', that is, a whipping thread is taken down the right-hand side and along the bottom to prevent the unsecured stitches from slipping in the mesh. This whipping stitch is taken into the darning over a bar,

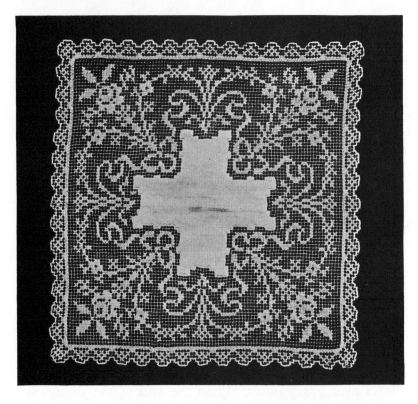

Fig. 20.—A square mat of filet lace

and behind the next bar running at right angles to the one already overstitched. The start and finish of all darning threads is made with a small reef knot. Some specimens of filet are darning with a weaving stitch working in one direction only, but this is not usual.

128

DESIGNS

Filet designs vary tremendously in character, ranging from gay little floral motifs and borders and geometrical arrangements to complete pictorial effects, embodying figures of human beings and animals, birds, buildings and trees. The designs are copied from a chart. There are innumerable books of patterns suitable for this work; alternatively charts prepared for cross-stitch or crochet are excellent substitutes. When making her own net the worker should always ascertain by counting the requisite number of squares if this is large enough to accommodate the design.

MATERIALS

The choice of these entirely depends on the texture of the lace to be made. The sizes of mesh, netting needle and thread should be relative to each other. A bone or steel pin, size 12, is equivalent to a quarter-inch mesh, a number 15 needle to an eighth of an inch mesh, and a number 17 needle to a sixteenth of an inch mesh. This last would only be used for a fine lace, as it makes a mesh of approximately eleven squares to the inch.

The netting needle should be of such a size that it would pass easily through the stitches. For the same reason it is not advisable to wind too much thread at one time, or the added bulk protruding from the sides of the netting needle will stretch the stitches out of place.

The thread should be of suitable thickness for the

required mesh, a good twisted crochet cotton or linen thread being recommended. The design is usually darned with the same thread, but some workers advocate a finer number, while others obtain bolder effects with less tedious darning by using a coarser thread.

For making the net a stirrup will be required. This consists of a longish loop of tape or string on which to work the first meshes. The loop should be made steady either by passing it under the foot or by hanging it to a convenient knob, hook or arm of a chair. However fixed, the stirrup should be of a length that, when pulled taut, it reaches a comfortable working position in the worker's hand.

When darning in the design the net is mounted on the square metal frame, padded with a piece of binding to prevent the lacing threads slipping. Overstitch the edge of the mesh over the sides of the frame, drawing up as tightly as possible. The darning should be done with a blunt-pointed needle.

METHOD OF NETTING

Wind the netting needle and arrange the stirrup at a comfortable angle. Either tie a small foundation loop to the stirrup or work directly into it. Tie the free end of the working thread to the loop or stirrup. Take the mesh in the left hand and hold it horizontally under the starting knot. Pass the thread over the mesh and round the second and third fingers of the left hand, bring it back across the first finger holding it in place with the thumb, between the first finger and the mesh (see Diagram XXXI). From the thumb carry the thread upwards to the right towards the stirrup; bring the thread down behind the mesh and behind all the fingers. Now pass the shuttle with the point away from you through the first loop between the mesh and the first finger, on through the foundation

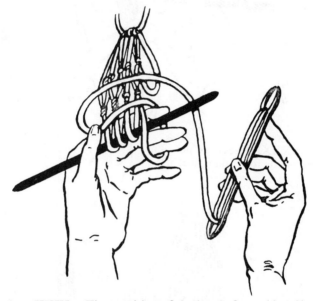

Diagram XXXI.—First position of the hands for making filet net

loop, and over the working thread which should still be lying slack between the thumb and the shuttle top (see Diagram XXXII).

Hold the mesh still and tighten the working thread so that it forms a loop under the little finger of the left hand. Still pulling on the working thread drop the first loop from under the thumb (see Diagram

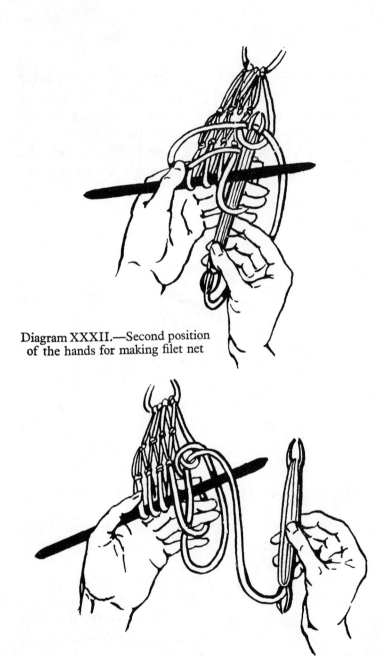

Diagram XXXII.—Second position
of the hands for making filet net

Diagram XXXIII.—Third position of the hands for making filet net

XXXIII). Next drop the loop from the second and third fingers and with the aid of the loop round the little finger tighten the thread round the mesh, draw it as tightly as possible, release the loop from the little finger, and pull the knot close. Repeat this stitch as many times as required. If the number of worked stitches cannot be comfortably accommodated on the mesh a few could be removed from the left-hand side to make room for the new ones. When the row is complete withdraw the mesh, turn the net over so that the thread is again on the left-hand side. Place the mesh immediately below the loops of the preceding row and proceed as before, working into each loop in turn. This principle covers net-making as a whole. To make the square-meshed net peculiar to filet lace proceed as follows: Commence at one corner of the net and work diagonally, increasing at every row. Begin by working two stitches into the foundation loop, turn the work and make one stitch into the first loop and two into the second. Turn again and work one stitch into each loop and two into the last. Continue in this way until there is a sufficient number of stitches to form half the required square. If counting the number of meshes for a given pattern, allow one extra stitch from the needle. Now work one row without increase and complete the square by decreasing at the end of each row. This is done by working two loops into the last stitch. When two stitches only remain, break the working thread and knot both loops together with the loose end. Remove the stirrup and tie the first two stitches in like manner.

To work an oblong, make the net to the required width, as for a square. Then work one row plain. In the next row decrease, and in the following one, increase. Work these two rows alternately until the

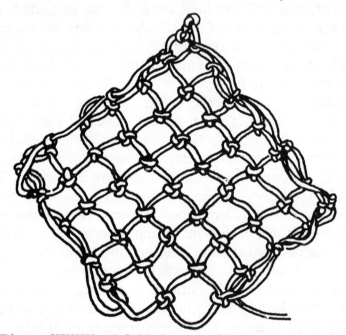

Diagram XXXIV.—A finished square of filet net, before the last two meshes are tied

required length is obtained. Then finish, as for the second half of a square.

A vandyke edging is commenced at a corner with two stitches, and increased in the usual way until there are say seven stitches on the mesh (the depth of the lace may be increased as desired). Work one row without increase; in the next row increase at the end.

Work a plain row and an increased row alternately until the mesh holds ten loops. After the last increase and turn, netting seven stitches only and leaving three unworked. Repeat from the star to any length required.

An alternative method of making a vandyke or other shaped edge is very simple. Make a piece of net twice as wide as required, and buttonhole the vandyke shape along the centre of the piece, taking one or two stitches into each mesh. Turn the work the other way up and follow the shape on the opposite bars of the same mesh. You now have two rows of stitching, working one up into the other. By cutting through the centre of the bars between the two rows you will have two strips of edged net. If desired any number of strips can thus be arranged and worked on a sufficiently large piece of net.

The edges of net insertions and lace should be firmly and closely buttonholed to add strength and weight. If a motif is being made for insertion it may be attached to the linen with this stitch.

Should it be necessary to cut an edge for any purpose, it should be held with a loose buttonhole of one stitch into each mesh, this being enough to prevent strain on the severed bars.

The net is now ready for the design, which is darned in the manner previously described. To the worker who is conversant with the more intricate needle-run stitches, this is exceedingly simple.

CHAPTER X

TATTING

IT was not originally intended to include Tatting in this book for it must be admitted it is, like Irish Crochet, something of an interloper. However, the revival of this lovely lace-like work together with a daily increasing demand for more information on the subject makes it impossible to omit it altogether, especially as it has at one time or another been successfully combined with nearly all the foregoing methods of lace-making. Space only permits of a very brief sketch of the working methods, but this should be sufficient to enable the interested learner to master the craft, after which it is a simple matter either to obtain written instructions or to devise original designs.

Once a most popular type of hand-work, Tatting has during the last quarter of a century been almost a dead art in this country, although in France the French version Frivolité has continued to enjoy popularity. Of late a revived interest in Tatting has shown itself on this side of the Channel.

The work is done with a single thread which is wound on a shuttle and with the aid of this knotted over the fingers to form lacy patterns that are very lovely when worked in fine threads. Once the knack has been acquired the work is quick and easy as it is composed of only two stitches worked alternately.

The finished work can be used in several ways. As a fine edging, motifs or insertions it may be worked alone or in conjunction with crochet or needle-point fillings. For dainty accessories, small tray-cloths or table-mats, it may be used as borders or mounted on net. In the latter case some lovely effects can be obtained by introducing needle-run stitches.

DESIGNS

Tatting designs are all based on different arrangements of the little rings of knotted stitches seen in Specimen I, 1. These are made with or without picots. If the rings are joined this must be done through a picot stitch. Other variations can be made by working with two threads and two shuttles, or by using one only of the usual double knots. When two shuttles are used the design may be worked out in two colours with very charming results.

When the knot has been mastered it is comparatively easy to build up simple designs. For anything more complicated the worker can obtain clearly written instructions similar to those given for crochet.

The usual abbreviations given in these are D. or D.S. for the double-knotted stitch, P. for a Picot, and S.S. for a single stitch. L. usually indicates a loop and J. a join.

MATERIALS

The shuttle is the first consideration. This is formed of two blades usually of bone or tortoiseshell. These are joined in the centre by a short bar with a hole in it, forming a spool on which to wind the thread, the end being first tied through the hole. A well-shaped shuttle is a tremendous aid to quick even working. The blades should be very smooth and the slightly curved points should nearly touch so that the cotton will not unwind too quickly. The size is a matter for choice, depending largely on the thickness of the thread being used. An average size for a fairly fine thread is about 3 inches in length by three-quarters of an inch wide. Some of the older shuttles are much longer in comparison with the width. When winding the thread care should be taken to see that the spool is not too full. If there is a bulge of cotton protruding beyond the sides of the shuttle the thread will become rubbed and discoloured.

A well-twisted crochet cotton is the best material for ordinary use, but tatting can be done in any thread, flax, silk, cotton or even soft string. It is very effective when worked in colour although the usual lace shades are the most popular. In addition to the above equipment the worker will require a small steel crochet hook or as a substitute a long pin.

METHOD

The stitch is worked into a loop thus. Take the free end of the thread between the finger and thumb of the left hand and make a loop round all the fingers, holding it taut by extending the middle one. Bring the thread back to the starting-point, holding it firmly between the finger and thumb, crossing the loose end already held there (see Diagram XXXVA). This forms the ring into which the stitches are worked.

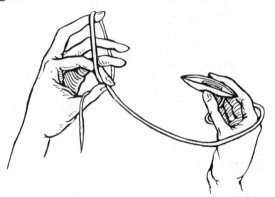

Diagram XXXVA.—First position of the hands

Now with the shuttle held in the right hand pass the thread over the back of that hand forming a second loop. Now work the shuttle under the thread of the

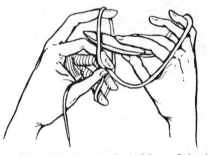

Diagram XXXVB.—Second position of the hands

first loop, back over the same thread, and through the loop made over the right hand (see Diagram XXXVI). Let the loop in the left hand go slack and tighten up the thread in the right hand. This will throw the twist of the stitch over so that it comes in the thread of the left-hand loop instead of in the right-hand

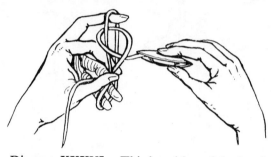

Diagram XXXVI.—Third position of the hands

working thread. This forms the first stitch of the double knot. The second stitch is made by allowing the working thread to hang loose instead of looped

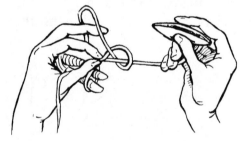

Diagram XXXVII.—Fourth position of the hands

over the right hand. The shuttle action is now reversed, working first over and then under the left-hand loop and back through the hanging loop. The stitch is pulled up as before. These two stitches compose the double knot used throughout all tatting designs. To test if

140

the knot is correctly pulled up see if the working thread runs easily. If the twist is not turned over in the right way the working thread will become fixed and fail to draw up when necessary.

When a certain number of stitches are worked the right-hand thread is drawn up tightly to form a ring or oval loop. A short length of thread, say a quarter of an inch, is then left and another loop made over the left hand and the process repeated. This makes the simple edging shown in Specimen I, 1.

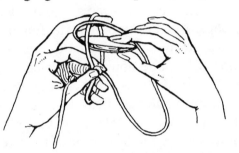

Diagram XXXVIII.—Fifth position of the hands

To form a picot stitch leave the head of the stitch about a quarter of an inch long instead of pulling it up tightly, but turn the knot as usual. Thus when the working thread is drawn up the loose-headed or picot stitches protrude beyond the others.

When two loops are to be joined this is done through the picot (see instructions for Specimen I, 2). The addition of picot stitches at frequent intervals considerably lightens and improves the appearance of the lace.

Tatting with two threads enables the worker to

141

make two scalloped edges for an insertion, and also enables her to make a straight or curved bar which is specially useful in straight edgings.

To join on a new shuttleful of thread, tie the old length to the new in a tight close knot as near to the base of a loop as possible.

Specimen I, 1. Work twelve double stitches into a loop, draw up, leave a quarter of an inch of thread, make another loop and work twelve more double stitches. Proceed in this manner to the required length.

Specimen I, 2. This illustrates a join made through the picot loops. Make a loop over the fingers as before, working into it four doubles and one picot, three doubles, one picot, one double, one picot, one double, one picot, three doubles, one picot, four doubles. Draw this up into an oval. Leave a quarter of an inch of thread, and make another loop as follows. Three doubles, now join to the last picot of the previous loop by drawing the working thread through the picot with a pin or crochet hook and passing the shuttle from right to left through the loop so formed. This should in no way interfere with the drawing up of the second loop. Proceed with the second loop working two doubles, one picot, two doubles, one picot, three doubles, and draw up. Work the first loop again, but omit the first picot, joining at this point to the last picot of the previous pattern. These loops are repeated alternately to the required length.

Specimen I, 3. This illustrates how Tatting can be formed into an attractive motif. Work a circle alternating two doubles, with one picot, until there are eight

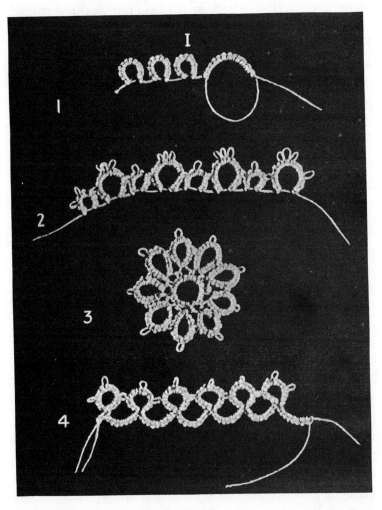

Fig. 21.—Sampler I, in large specimens, showing the principles of
Tatting

143

picots on the ring. Draw up and tie the working thread
to the first stitch thus forming a ninth picot. Do not
break the working thread. With this ring as a base
loop the working thread again and work four doubles,
one picot, four doubles, one picot, four doubles, one
picot, four doubles and draw up. Join the base of this
loop to the first picot on the ring. Work a second
loop in the same way but join twice. First to the last

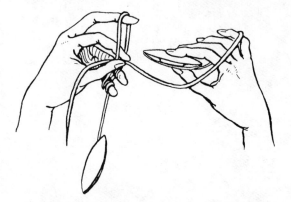

Diagram XXXIX.—Using two shuttles

picot of the previous loop and when complete to the
second picot of the centre ring. This is repeated until
the centre ring is surrounded by loops. The thread
may then be broken and a new star commenced, or
the rose may be continued for another round, increasing the size of the motif. Alternatively such motifs
may be joined in a line by the side picots.

Specimen I, 4. This shows the working of two
shuttles (see Diagram XXXIX). If more convenient a
reel may be used in place of the second shuttle. Tie

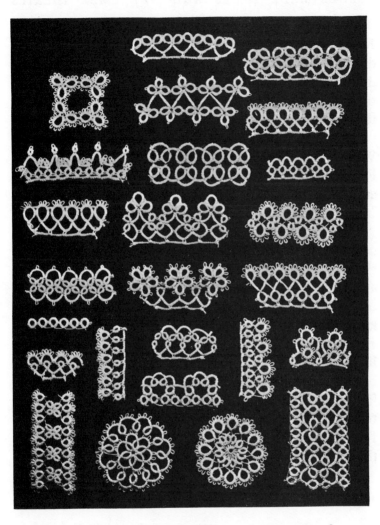

Fig. 22A.—Small motifs and edgings in Tatting, taken from
an old sampler

the two loose ends together and let one shuttle hang. Make a loop with the other, working into it four doubles, one picot, four doubles, one picot, four doubles, one picot, four doubles. Draw up. Reverse the work, holding it by the pattern just made. Take the second thread over the hand to form a loop, twisting the end round the little finger to steady it. Work nine doubles into this with the first shuttle. Reverse the work again, dropping the second thread and repeating the first loop with the first thread only. Join the patterns of the upper loops by the side picots.

Other variations of the stitch are Josephine knots composed of six or seven single stitches drawn up tightly; Bullion knots made by passing the shuttle over and over a loop any number of times and drawing it up to form a stitch, somewhat similar to a French knot; and dots composed of five or six doubles not too closely drawn, so that they lie flat to form a tiny shell-like edging. These variations are more often found on old specimens of work than on modern pieces. The Tatting samplers, be it noted, are worked out in string to enable the worker to follow the design more closely. For the real Tatting effects it is necessary to refer to the photographs of edgings and motifs.

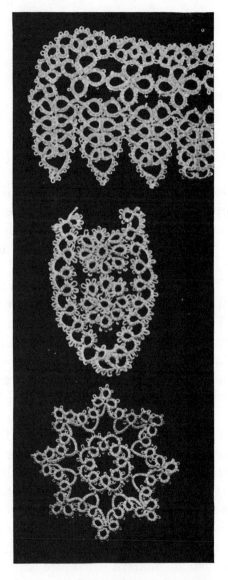

Fig. 22B.— Small motifs and edgings in Tatting, taken from
an old sampler

147

CHAPTER XI

MODERN ADAPTATIONS OF NEEDLE-MADE LACES AND NET DARNING

EVERY few years the fashions in both furnishings and wearing apparel change completely. Therefore unless a given type of needle-craft keeps step with the march of time it soon falls into disfavour and finally into disuse.

It is our responsibility, all of us who love this craft, to see that this does not happen to our priceless heritage. We must therefore take all that has been given us in the past, moulding it to suit the needs of the present.

How can this best be done? Let us see first what are the needs of a modern household. The fashion for plate-glass tops for tables and trays has created a demand for exceedingly dainty cloths and coverings, the fragility of which is adequately protected by the glass. What could be more suitable for this purpose than some of the lace-work described in earlier chapters made up in suitable modern shapes? The worker would be well advised to make her choice from Princess, needle-point or needle-run varieties.

Highly-polished modern furniture calls for some slight protection, although anything too heavy would spoil its beauty. Some of the many coloured squared curtain nets make ideal runners and utility mats, especially if embroidered with the needle-run outlining and filling stitches. If done in colour some of this work is exceedingly attractive.

Modern houses are frequently overlooked, making adequate window-screens necessary. Something really original can be evolved by working curtain nets in modern designs, embroidered with lace stitches. One such curtain recently exhibited depicted a complete under-sea scene carried out as a wide border, coming at the height of the sill on a full-length curtain. The water was shaded in blues and greens and worked diagonally on the net in simple darning stitch. Tropical fish and coral of vivid hues were worked in such stitches as appear in Limerick lace. A few strands of sober-coloured seaweed added balance and character to the design. It was a curtain of which one would never tire, for every time the breezes moved it the fish seemed to leap to life and swim within their silken sea.

Another charming curtain arrangement which appeared during the spring months was a short net blind gathered into a straight net band which displayed a border of gay crocuses in natural colours, the stitch used being simple darning.

Another practical piece of work designed to protect very light upholstery was based on Carrickmacross lace, the net ground being represented by coarse curtain net and the muslin by strong cream linen. This was appliquéd with a buttonhole stitch and no fancy stitches were introduced.

Most attractive cushions and day pillows to go with

less severe furnishings can be arranged with Point, Filet or Reticella laces. The latter is so popular at the present time that much is being produced by machine for use as table mats and cloths of all sizes. Although some of this work is very pleasing it is not to be compared with hand embroidery and the discriminating worker will never regret time spent on making such lovely additions to her linen cupboard.

Lingerie accessories are back in favour again. Not quite in the old floppy style of the 'nineties, but neat well-tailored effects that can nevertheless be most attractive in well-made lace. For this purpose Tatting is becoming exceedingly popular.

Another charming fashion for trimming house linen is the insertion of small filet squares, darned with an initial or monogram.

These are only a few adaptations planned by enterprising needle-women, but they suffice to illustrate the ways in which workers of originality can serve their generation.

CHAPTER XII

THE CARE OF LACE

EVERY lace lover, be her preference for the ancient or the modern, should learn to care for her treasure.

LACE FUNGUS

The first and deadliest enemy of lace is fungus. This disease attacks the lace when it becomes damp or lies too long in the same folds. It is exceedingly catching and will, if not checked, soon spread through a whole pile of lace. It appears like tiny spots of iron mould or rust, which are by the uninitiated often attributed to old pin-marks. At the first sign of such spots they should be immediately treated. If the disease is very bad the affected part should be cut out and replaced. In the case of a cotton or linen thread lace, the part may be treated with chemicals, but as infinite harm may be done in this way it is wiser to consult an expert.

To prevent an attack by fungus all specimens of lace not in regular use should be kept in folds of blue or black tissue-paper. Every few months they should be shaken out for an hour or so in a warm place, preferably in the sun and air. When they are repacked avoid folding in the same creases.

TO WASH LACE

Most people are dreadfully afraid to trust old lace to soap and water, but in the writer's opinion this is a harmless treatment compared with some of the dry-cleaning methods advocated, since most of these require the use of some chemical.

If the lace is extremely old and fragile or of great value, it should be handed over to an expert. A great deal of dirt can be removed by soaking in cold water, and this is the best preliminary cleanser. It should be followed by a good lather of soft soap or soap flakes. Care is required to see that every particle of soap is melted, otherwise it will stick in the meshes and look unsightly when dry. In order to prevent this it is safer to bring the lather to the boil and then let it cool before immersing the lace. Rubbing should be avoided at all costs, as this weakens the threads. Press the lace gently between the hands until clean, and then rinse in tepid water. An alternative method is to put both the lace and the lather into a wide-necked bottling jar, replacing the screw top, and shaking the bottle well. If this is not sufficient to remove the dirt, the lace may be placed in an earthen jar or double-boiler, prefer-ably not metal, and brought to the boil for a few minutes. It is not advisable to boil very old and tender lace, but in most cases it will do no harm. If a piece of fragile lace is very dirty and greasy it may be soaked in olive oil for a few days. This loosens the dirt and feeds the thread, making it easier to handle. After the oil bath the lace should be washed in the usual way.

Fig. 23.—Method of drying lace, showing the edges pulled out
on supporting pins

It is well worth while to dry lace properly no matter what its value, for edges correctly pinned out will have a crispness and newness never to be obtained by merely pulling or ironing them.

A board or old table-top covered with linen should be used for drying. The lace is then pinned out as shown in the illustration. Fine steel pins should be used and the main units of the design drawn into place and fixed. After this each small picot is pulled out and pinned and the board set in a warm place until the lace is perfectly dry. When the pins are removed it will be seen to have regained most of its original loveliness.

If the lace appears very tender it may be pinned out before washing and dabbed, but never rubbed, with a soap sponge. The rinsing is done in the same way with clear tepid water.

Should lace require stiffening use a little water in which rice has been boiled. This is smoother than starch and gives body to the lace without making it harsh.

To tint lace use a little tea or coffee. This must be strained through a very fine muslin to prevent any leaves or grounds getting on to the lace and so dyeing it in dark spots. Tea gives a rather pinker tone than coffee. Either can be used at any strength according to the shade required. A test can be made with a scrap of net or muslin.

LACE MENDING

Mending often presents a problem. If the specimen is very valuable it should be put into skilled hands, but simple repairs can easily be executed at home. Diagrams XL, XLI and XLII show how a piece of torn net may be renovated.

Bars are usually the first part of point lace to show wear. These can be renewed with a thread and stitch as near the original as possible. Instructions for making the most common bars appear elsewhere in this book.

Many very old specimens of point lace where the ground has worn beyond repair have been successfully appliquéd on to net. Small pillow lace motifs or braid motifs can be remounted in the same way when the original ground has rotted. It is often possible to re-fashion a piece of lace entirely by cutting a differently shaped net pattern and appliquéing the old units thereon.

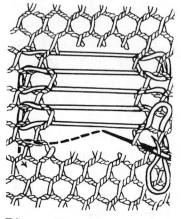 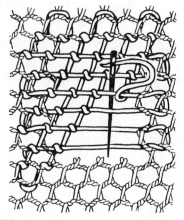

Diagram XL.—Net mending (*a*)   Diagram XLI.—Net mending (*b*)

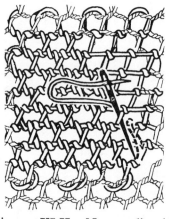

Diagram XLII.—Net mending (*c*)

GLOSSARY OF THE COMMONER LACE TERMS

Bar. The thread surrounding the hole in net.

Brides. The 'bridges' or connecting bars in both needle-point and bobbin lace. These can be made in various ways.

Caskets. Term used in needle-run laces for the spaces to be ornamented with filling stitches.

Cordonnet. The raised or thickened outline of the design. Usually worked in a thicker thread than the filling, or alternatively worked over in a whip, buttonhole or over-cast to bring it up in relief.

Fillings. A simple term describing the fancy stitches used to 'fill' or embellish the design. These are many and varied, the different groupings making tiny designs within themselves. A lace specimen of doubtful origin may often be classified by these stitches. The same term applies alike to needle-run, needle-point and bobbin laces.

Grounds. The background on which the design is built. The term applies alike to the nets in needle-run, and the brides used in needle-point.

Guipure. A term applied to any lace having a running tape-like design connected with needle-made brides.

Mesh. The hole. Thus in describing a stitch we say 'under one mesh and two bars' or 'under one bar and into a mesh'.

Picots. The little decorative loops used to adorn plain 'brides', or edgings.

'Toile' or 'Gimp'. The design as distinct from the ground. 'Gimp' is more often used for a modern machine-made edging.

INDEX

ABBREVIATIONS (Tatting), 137
Adaptations of Lace, 148, 149, 155
Anne of Bohemia, 17
Appliqué, Carrickmacross, 25, 65

BARS:
Guipure, 76, 77
Irish Crochet, 92
Needle-point, 114
Buttonholed, 105
Double-sided Buttonhole, 106
Buttonholed with Thorn, 119, 122
Whipped, 104
Woven, 105
Reticella, 104, 105, 106
Basket Stitch (see Pyramid Stitch), 43, 44
Braids:
Battenberg, 114
Bruges, 114
Flemish, 114
Honiton, 19, 110, 114
Point, 114
Russian, 114
Brides (see Bars)
Buckinghamshire Lace, 19
Bullion Knots, 146
Buttonhole Stitches, 49, 103, 105, 106, 120, 122, 124

CARE of Lace, 151
Carrickmacross:
Appliqué, 24, 25, 65–73
Guipure, 24, 25, 68, 69, 70
Caskets, 22, 53, 54, 55, 56, 57, 58
Catherine de Medicis, 18
Cobweb Stitch, 41, 42, 55
Coggeshall Lace, 22, 30
Cording Carrickmacross, 65, 66, 67, 68, 72, 73
Cording Irish Crochet, 82, 85–93
Cordonnet, 66
Crochet, Irish, 25, 81–94
Cut-work, 16, 95

DESIGN :
Braid Point, 26, 114
Carrickmacross, 25, 70
Filet, 27, 129
Irish Crochet, 25, 81
Needle-run, 22, 36
Princess, 27, 108
Reticella, 26, 97
Tatting, 28, 137
Devonshire Point, 26, 114
Drying Lace, 153, 154
Duchess Lace, 108, 114

EDGINGS:
Buttonholed, 40, 68, 105
Irish Crochet, 94
Filet, 127, 134, 135
Machine-made, 21, 117
Reticella, 99

FAN Stitch, 125
Fancy Satin Stitch, 45
Feather Stitch, 75
Fern Leaves, 90
Figure Eight Stitch, 51, 74
Fil de Trace, 97, 98, 99
Filet Lace, 27, 129
Fillings (see Stitches)
Fixing:
Carrickmacross, 65–68
Filet, 127
Irish Crochet, 82, 83
Modern Needle-point, 116
Needle-run, 30–36
Princess, 108, 110, 112
Reticella, 97–102
Tambour, 60
Flemish Lace, 19
Flemish Point, 114
Flemish Lace Stitch, 125
Framing:
Needle-run, 30, 32
Frivolité, 28, 137
Fungus on Lace, 151

158

INDEX

Genoa Lace Stitch, 124, 126
Gimp (see Machine-made Edgings)
Grey Porter, Mrs., 24
Grounds:
    Brussels, 19, 21
    Drawn Thread, 100
    Fil de Trace, 98, 99
    Irish Crochet (see Irish Crochet Bars)
    Point (see Needle-point Bars)

Heathcote, John, 21
Herringbone Stitch, 44
Honiton Lace, 19, 26
    Town of, 19

Industries, Lace: South Indian, Irish, Isle of Wight, etc., 22–24
Irish Crochet, 25, 26, 81–94
Irish Lace Industries, 22, 24, 25
Isle of Wight Lace, 22 (see Needle-run Lace), 30
Italian Lace, 24

Joining:
    Irish Crochet Units, 91
    Needle-run Patterns, 38
    Point Braids, 110
    Tatting by picot, 141
Josephine Knots, 146

Katherine of Aragon, 17
Knotted Stitch, 47, 57

Laces:
    Bobbin Lace (see Pillow Lace)
    Braid Point, 26
    Buckingham, 19
    Carrickmacross:
        Appliqué, 24, 25, 65–73
        Guipure, 24, 25, 68, 69, 70
    Coggeshall, 22, 30
    Duchess, 114
    Filet, 27, 129–135
    Flemish Point, 114
    Honiton, 19, 26
    Irish Point, 107
    Isle of Wight, 22, 30
    Italian, 24
    Lacis (see Filet)
    Limerick, 22

Laces (continued)
    Needle-made (see Needle-run and Needle-point)
    Needle-point, 26, 96, 126
    Needle-run, 21, 22
    Nottingham, 20
    Pillow Lace, 19
    Reticella, 26, 95–107
    Rose Point, 107
    Spanish, 25
    Tambour, 24, 59–64
    Venetian Point, 114
    Youghal, 107
Laced Stitch, 75
Limerick Lace, 22

Machine-made Net, 20, 21
Makouk (see Tatting)
Mary of Scotland, 17
Mary Steadman, 24
Materials:
    Filet, 129
    Irish Crochet, 83
    Needle-run Laces, 39
    Point Laces, 26, 27, 107, 114, 126
    Reticella, 102
    Tatting, 137
Meshes, repairing (see Net), 156
    shapes of, 20
    substitutes for, 129
Methods:
    Carrickmacross, 15
    Filet, 127
    Irish Crochet, 81
    Limerick, 30
    Point Lace, 114
    Princess, 108
    Tambour, 59
    Tatting, 136

Needle-point, 26, 114, 126
Needle-point Fillings (see Stitches)
Needle-run, 22, 30–58
Needle-run Fillings (see Stitches)
Net:
    Darning, 127 (see Needle-run Stitches)
    Hand-made (see Filet), 130, 134
    Machine-made, 121
    Repairing, 156
Netting (see Hand-made Net)
Netting Needles, 129

Occhi (see Tatting)

159

INDEX

PETALLED Flower (*see* Irish Crochet)
Picot:
  as Machine-made Edging (*see* Gimp), 117
  in Carrickmacross, 72
  in Tatting, 141
Pillow Lace, 19
Point Braids, 114
Point d'Espagne, 125
Point Lace, 17, 95, 114
Princess Lace, 108
Punto in aria, 16, 95
Pyramid Stitch, 120

REID of Rahans, Miss, 25
Renaissance Work, 27
Repairs, 155
Reticella, 26, 95–107
Riego de la Blanchardière, Mademoiselle, 25
Ring Stitch, 48, 54
Rings, 85
Rose (*see* Irish Crochet Units), 85, 86, 87
Rose Point, 107

SATIN Stitch Dots, 46
Shamrock (*see* Irish Crochet Units), 89
Shuttle, 137, 138
Slanting Crossed Stitch, 50
South Indian Lace Industry, 24
Spanish Lace, 25
Stirrup, 130
Stitches:
  Basket Stitch, 44
  Bullion Knots, 146
  Buttonholed Stitches, 49, 76, 103, 105, 106, 120, 122
  Cobweb Stitch, 42
  Fan Stitch, 125
  Feather Stitch, 75
  Figure Eight Stitch, 51, 53
  Flemish Lace Stitch, 125
  Genoa Lace Stitch, 126

Stitches (*continued*)
  Herringbone Stitch, 44
  Josephine Knots, 146
  Knotted Stitch, 47
  Overcasting or Whipped Stitch, 52
  Point d'Espagne, 125
  Pyramid, 120
  Ring Stitch, 48
  Satin Stitch Dots, Stars, Fancy, 45, 46
  Simple Lattice Stitch, 75
  Slanting Crossed Stitch, 50
  Tambour Stitch, 62, 63
  Tent Stitch, 42
  Twisted Filling Stitch, 123
  Veining Stitch, 121
  Wheel Stitch, 121

TAMBOUR, 23, 59–64
Tatting, 28, 136–146
Tent Stitch, 42
Thistle (*see* Irish Crochet Units), 89
Tinting Lace, 154
Toile, 20
Twisted Filling Stitches, 123

UNITS (Irish Crochet), 85–94
  Bars, 92
  Edgings, 92
  Fern, 90
  Petalled Flower, 87
  Rings, 85
  Roses (Large and Small), 85, 87
  Shamrock, 89
  Stems, 91
  Thistle, 89

VEILS, Wedding, 31, 35
Veining Stitch, 121

WASHING Lace, 152
Whipped Bars, 104
Whipped Stitch, 52

YOUGHAL, 107

A CATALOG OF SELECTED
DOVER BOOKS
IN ALL FIELDS OF INTEREST

A CATALOG OF SELECTED DOVER
BOOKS IN ALL FIELDS OF INTEREST

DRAWINGS OF REMBRANDT, edited by Seymour Slive. Updated Lippmann, Hofstede de Groot edition, with definitive scholarly apparatus. All portraits, biblical sketches, landscapes, nudes. Oriental figures, classical studies, together with selection of work by followers. 550 illustrations. Total of 630pp. 9⅛ × 12¼.
21485-0, 21486-9 Pa., Two-vol. set $25.00

GHOST AND HORROR STORIES OF AMBROSE BIERCE, Ambrose Bierce. 24 tales vividly imagined, strangely prophetic, and decades ahead of their time in technical skill: "The Damned Thing," "An Inhabitant of Carcosa," "The Eyes of the Panther," "Moxon's Master," and 20 more. 199pp. 5⅜ × 8½. 20767-6 Pa. $3.95

ETHICAL WRITINGS OF MAIMONIDES, Maimonides. Most significant ethical works of great medieval sage, newly translated for utmost precision, readability. Laws Concerning Character Traits, Eight Chapters, more. 192pp. 5⅜ × 8½.
24522-5 Pa. $4.50

THE EXPLORATION OF THE COLORADO RIVER AND ITS CANYONS, J. W. Powell. Full text of Powell's 1,000-mile expedition down the fabled Colorado in 1869. Superb account of terrain, geology, vegetation, Indians, famine, mutiny, treacherous rapids, mighty canyons, during exploration of last unknown part of continental U.S. 400pp. 5⅜ × 8½. 20094-9 Pa. $6.95

HISTORY OF PHILOSOPHY, Julián Marías. Clearest one-volume history on the market. Every major philosopher and dozens of others, to Existentialism and later. 505pp. 5⅜ × 8½. 21739-6 Pa. $8.50

ALL ABOUT LIGHTNING, Martin A. Uman. Highly readable non-technical survey of nature and causes of lightning, thunderstorms, ball lightning, St. Elmo's Fire, much more. Illustrated. 192pp. 5⅜ × 8½. 25237-X Pa. $5.95

SAILING ALONE AROUND THE WORLD, Captain Joshua Slocum. First man to sail around the world, alone, in small boat. One of great feats of seamanship told in delightful manner. 67 illustrations. 294pp. 5⅜ × 8½. 20326-3 Pa. $4.50

LETTERS AND NOTES ON THE MANNERS, CUSTOMS AND CONDI-TIONS OF THE NORTH AMERICAN INDIANS, George Catlin. Classic account of life among Plains Indians: ceremonies, hunt, warfare, etc. 312 plates. 572pp. of text. 6⅛ × 9¼. 22118-0, 22119-9 Pa. Two-vol. set $15.90

ALASKA: The Harriman Expedition, 1899, John Burroughs, John Muir, et al. Informative, engrossing accounts of two-month, 9,000-mile expedition. Native peoples, wildlife, forests, geography, salmon industry, glaciers, more. Profusely illustrated. 240 black-and-white line drawings. 124 black-and-white photographs. 3 maps. Index. 576pp. 5⅜ × 8½. 25109-8 Pa. $11.95

THE BOOK OF BEASTS: Being a Translation from a Latin Bestiary of the Twelfth Century, T. H. White. Wonderful catalog real and fanciful beasts: manticore, griffin, phoenix, amphivius, jaculus, many more. White's witty erudite commentary on scientific, historical aspects. Fascinating glimpse of medieval mind. Illustrated. 296pp. 5⅜ × 8¼. (Available in U.S. only) 24609-4 Pa. $5.95

FRANK LLOYD WRIGHT: ARCHITECTURE AND NATURE With 160 Illustrations, Donald Hoffmann. Profusely illustrated study of influence of nature—especially prairie—on Wright's designs for Fallingwater, Robie House, Guggenheim Museum, other masterpieces. 96pp. 9¼ × 10¾. 25098-9 Pa. $7.95

FRANK LLOYD WRIGHT'S FALLINGWATER, Donald Hoffmann. Wright's famous waterfall house: planning and construction of organic idea. History of site, owners, Wright's personal involvement. Photographs of various stages of building. Preface by Edgar Kaufmann, Jr. 100 illustrations. 112pp. 9¼ × 10. 23671-4 Pa. $7.95

YEARS WITH FRANK LLOYD WRIGHT: Apprentice to Genius, Edgar Tafel. Insightful memoir by a former apprentice presents a revealing portrait of Wright the man, the inspired teacher, the greatest American architect. 372 black-and-white illustrations. Preface. Index. vi + 228pp. 8¼ × 11. 24801-1 Pa. $9.95

THE STORY OF KING ARTHUR AND HIS KNIGHTS, Howard Pyle. Enchanting version of King Arthur fable has delighted generations with imaginative narratives of exciting adventures and unforgettable illustrations by the author. 41 illustrations. xviii + 313pp. 6⅛ × 9¼. 21445-1 Pa. $5.95

THE GODS OF THE EGYPTIANS, E. A. Wallis Budge. Thorough coverage of numerous gods of ancient Egypt by foremost Egyptologist. Information on evolution of cults, rites and gods; the cult of Osiris; the Book of the Dead and its rites; the sacred animals and birds; Heaven and Hell; and more. 956pp. 6⅛ × 9¼. 22055-9, 22056-7 Pa., Two-vol. set $20.00

A THEOLOGICO-POLITICAL TREATISE, Benedict Spinoza. Also contains unfinished *Political Treatise*. Great classic on religious liberty, theory of government on common consent. R. Elwes translation. Total of 421pp. 5⅜ × 8½. 20249-6 Pa. $6.95

INCIDENTS OF TRAVEL IN CENTRAL AMERICA, CHIAPAS, AND YUCATAN, John L. Stephens. Almost single-handed discovery of Maya culture; exploration of ruined cities, monuments, temples; customs of Indians. 115 drawings. 892pp. 5⅜ × 8½. 22404-X, 22405-8 Pa., Two-vol. set $15.90

LOS CAPRICHOS, Francisco Goya. 80 plates of wild, grotesque monsters and caricatures. Prado manuscript included. 183pp. 6⅛ × 9⅜. 22384-1 Pa. $4.95

AUTOBIOGRAPHY: The Story of My Experiments with Truth, Mohandas K. Gandhi. Not hagiography, but Gandhi in his own words. Boyhood, legal studies, purification, the growth of the Satyagraha (nonviolent protest) movement. Critical, inspiring work of the man who freed India. 480pp. 5⅜ × 8½. (Available in U.S. only) 24593-4 Pa. $6.95

ILLUSTRATED DICTIONARY OF HISTORIC ARCHITECTURE, edited by Cyril M. Harris. Extraordinary compendium of clear, concise definitions for over 5,000 important architectural terms complemented by over 2,000 line drawings. Covers full spectrum of architecture from ancient ruins to 20th-century Modernism. Preface. 592pp. 7½ × 9⅝. 24444-X Pa. $14.95

THE NIGHT BEFORE CHRISTMAS, Clement Moore. Full text, and woodcuts from original 1848 book. Also critical, historical material. 19 illustrations. 40pp. 4⅝ × 6. 22797-9 Pa. $2.25

THE LESSON OF JAPANESE ARCHITECTURE: 165 Photographs, Jiro Harada. Memorable gallery of 165 photographs taken in the 1930's of exquisite Japanese homes of the well-to-do and historic buildings. 13 line diagrams. 192pp. 8⅜ × 11¼. 24778-3 Pa. $8.95

THE AUTOBIOGRAPHY OF CHARLES DARWIN AND SELECTED LETTERS, edited by Francis Darwin. The fascinating life of eccentric genius composed of an intimate memoir by Darwin (intended for his children); commentary by his son, Francis; hundreds of fragments from notebooks, journals, papers; and letters to and from Lyell, Hooker, Huxley, Wallace and Henslow. xi + 365pp. 5⅜ × 8. 20479-0 Pa. $5.95

WONDERS OF THE SKY: Observing Rainbows, Comets, Eclipses, the Stars and Other Phenomena, Fred Schaaf. Charming, easy-to-read poetic guide to all manner of celestial events visible to the naked eye. Mock suns, glories, Belt of Venus, more. Illustrated. 299pp. 5¼ × 8¼. 24402-4 Pa. $7.95

BURNHAM'S CELESTIAL HANDBOOK, Robert Burnham, Jr. Thorough guide to the stars beyond our solar system. Exhaustive treatment. Alphabetical by constellation: Andromeda to Cetus in Vol. 1; Chamaeleon to Orion in Vol. 2; and Pavo to Vulpecula in Vol. 3. Hundreds of illustrations. Index in Vol. 3. 2,000pp. 6⅛ × 9¼. 23567-X, 23568-8, 23673-0 Pa., Three-vol. set $36.85

STAR NAMES: Their Lore and Meaning, Richard Hinckley Allen. Fascinating history of names various cultures have given to constellations and literary and folkloristic uses that have been made of stars. Indexes to subjects. Arabic and Greek names. Biblical references. Bibliography. 563pp. 5⅜ × 8½. 21079-0 Pa. $7.95

THIRTY YEARS THAT SHOOK PHYSICS: The Story of Quantum Theory, George Gamow. Lucid, accessible introduction to influential theory of energy and matter. Careful explanations of Dirac's anti-particles, Bohr's model of the atom, much more. 12 plates. Numerous drawings. 240pp. 5⅜ × 8½. 24895-X Pa. $4.95

CHINESE DOMESTIC FURNITURE IN PHOTOGRAPHS AND MEASURED DRAWINGS, Gustav Ecke. A rare volume, now affordably priced for antique collectors, furniture buffs and art historians. Detailed review of styles ranging from early Shang to late Ming. Unabridged republication. 161 black-and-white drawings, photos. Total of 224pp. 8⅜ × 11¼. (Available in U.S. only) 25171-3 Pa. $12.95

VINCENT VAN GOGH: A Biography, Julius Meier-Graefe. Dynamic, penetrating study of artist's life, relationship with brother, Theo, painting techniques, travels, more. Readable, engrossing. 160pp. 5⅜ × 8½. (Available in U.S. only) 25253-1 Pa. $3.95

HOW TO WRITE, Gertrude Stein. Gertrude Stein claimed anyone could understand her unconventional writing—here are clues to help. Fascinating improvisations, language experiments, explanations illuminate Stein's craft and the art of writing. Total of 414pp. 4⅝ × 6⅜. 23144-5 Pa. $5.95

ADVENTURES AT SEA IN THE GREAT AGE OF SAIL: Five Firsthand Narratives, edited by Elliot Snow. Rare true accounts of exploration, whaling, shipwreck, fierce natives, trade, shipboard life, more. 33 illustrations. Introduction. 353pp. 5⅜ × 8½. 25177-2 Pa. $7.95

THE HERBAL OR GENERAL HISTORY OF PLANTS, John Gerard. Classic descriptions of about 2,850 plants—with over 2,700 illustrations—includes Latin and English names, physical descriptions, varieties, time and place of growth, more. 2,706 illustrations. xlv + 1,678pp. 8½ × 12¼. 23147-X Cloth. $75.00

DOROTHY AND THE WIZARD IN OZ, L. Frank Baum. Dorothy and the Wizard visit the center of the Earth, where people are vegetables, glass houses grow and Oz characters reappear. Classic sequel to *Wizard of Oz*. 256pp. 5⅜ × 8.
24714-7 Pa. $4.95

SONGS OF EXPERIENCE: Facsimile Reproduction with 26 Plates in Full Color, William Blake. This facsimile of Blake's original "Illuminated Book" reproduces 26 full-color plates from a rare 1826 edition. Includes "The Tyger," "London," "Holy Thursday," and other immortal poems. 26 color plates. Printed text of poems. 48pp. 5¼ × 7. 24636-1 Pa. $3.50

SONGS OF INNOCENCE, William Blake. The first and most popular of Blake's famous "Illuminated Books," in a facsimile edition reproducing all 31 brightly colored plates. Additional printed text of each poem. 64pp. 5¼ × 7.
22764-2 Pa. $3.50

PRECIOUS STONES, Max Bauer. Classic, thorough study of diamonds, rubies, emeralds, garnets, etc.: physical character, occurrence, properties, use, similar topics. 20 plates, 8 in color. 94 figures. 659pp. 6⅛ × 9¼.
21910-0, 21911-9 Pa., Two-vol. set $14.90

ENCYCLOPEDIA OF VICTORIAN NEEDLEWORK, S. F. A. Caulfeild and Blanche Saward. Full, precise descriptions of stitches, techniques for dozens of needlecrafts—most exhaustive reference of its kind. Over 800 figures. Total of 679pp. 8⅛ × 11. Two volumes. Vol. 1 22800-2 Pa. $10.95
Vol. 2 22801-0 Pa. $10.95

THE MARVELOUS LAND OF OZ, L. Frank Baum. Second Oz book, the Scarecrow and Tin Woodman are back with hero named Tip, Oz magic. 136 illustrations. 287pp. 5⅜ × 8½. 20692-0 Pa. $5.95

WILD FOWL DECOYS, Joel Barber. Basic book on the subject, by foremost authority and collector. Reveals history of decoy making and rigging, place in American culture, different kinds of decoys, how to make them, and how to use them. 140 plates. 156pp. 7⅞ × 10¾. 20011-6 Pa. $7.95

HISTORY OF LACE, Mrs. Bury Palliser. Definitive, profusely illustrated chronicle of lace from earliest times to late 19th century. Laces of Italy, Greece, England, France, Belgium, etc. Landmark of needlework scholarship. 266 illustrations. 672pp. 6⅛ × 9¼. 24742-2 Pa. $14.95

ILLUSTRATED GUIDE TO SHAKER FURNITURE, Robert Meader. All furniture and appurtenances, with much on unknown local styles. 235 photos. 146pp. 9 × 12.   22819-3 Pa. $7.95

WHALE SHIPS AND WHALING: A Pictorial Survey, George Francis Dow. Over 200 vintage engravings, drawings, photographs of barks, brigs, cutters, other vessels. Also harpoons, lances, whaling guns, many other artifacts. Comprehensive text by foremost authority. 207 black-and-white illustrations. 288pp. 6 × 9.
24808-9 Pa. $8.95

THE BERTRAMS, Anthony Trollope. Powerful portrayal of blind self-will and thwarted ambition includes one of Trollope's most heartrending love stories. 497pp. 5⅜ × 8½.   25119-5 Pa. $8.95

ADVENTURES WITH A HAND LENS, Richard Headstrom. Clearly written guide to observing and studying flowers and grasses, fish scales, moth and insect wings, egg cases, buds, feathers, seeds, leaf scars, moss, molds, ferns, common crystals, etc.—all with an ordinary, inexpensive magnifying glass. 209 exact line drawings aid in your discoveries. 220pp. 5⅜ × 8½.   23330-8 Pa. $3.95

RODIN ON ART AND ARTISTS, Auguste Rodin. Great sculptor's candid, wide-ranging comments on meaning of art; great artists; relation of sculpture to poetry, painting, music; philosophy of life, more. 76 superb black-and-white illustrations of Rodin's sculpture, drawings and prints. 119pp. 8⅜ × 11¼.   24487-3 Pa. $6.95

FIFTY CLASSIC FRENCH FILMS, 1912–1982: A Pictorial Record, Anthony Slide. Memorable stills from Grand Illusion, Beauty and the Beast, Hiroshima, Mon Amour, many more. Credits, plot synopses, reviews, etc. 160pp. 8¼ × 11.
25256-6 Pa. $11.95

THE PRINCIPLES OF PSYCHOLOGY, William James. Famous long course complete, unabridged. Stream of thought, time perception, memory, experimental methods; great work decades ahead of its time. 94 figures. 1,391pp. 5⅜ × 8½.
20381-6, 20382-4 Pa., Two-vol. set $19.90

BODIES IN A BOOKSHOP, R. T. Campbell. Challenging mystery of blackmail and murder with ingenious plot and superbly drawn characters. In the best tradition of British suspense fiction. 192pp. 5⅜ × 8½.   24720-1 Pa. $3.95

CALLAS: PORTRAIT OF A PRIMA DONNA, George Jellinek. Renowned commentator on the musical scene chronicles incredible career and life of the most controversial, fascinating, influential operatic personality of our time. 64 black-and-white photographs. 416pp. 5⅜ × 8¼.   25047-4 Pa. $7.95

GEOMETRY, RELATIVITY AND THE FOURTH DIMENSION, Rudolph Rucker. Exposition of fourth dimension, concepts of relativity as Flatland characters continue adventures. Popular, easily followed yet accurate, profound. 141 illustrations. 133pp. 5⅜ × 8½.   23400-2 Pa. $3.50

HOUSEHOLD STORIES BY THE BROTHERS GRIMM, with pictures by Walter Crane. 53 classic stories—Rumpelstiltskin, Rapunzel, Hansel and Gretel, the Fisherman and his Wife, Snow White, Tom Thumb, Sleeping Beauty, Cinderella, and so much more—lavishly illustrated with original 19th century drawings. 114 illustrations. x + 269pp. 5⅜ × 8½.   21080-4 Pa. $4.50

SUNDIALS, Albert Waugh. Far and away the best, most thorough coverage of ideas, mathematics concerned, types, construction, adjusting anywhere. Over 100 illustrations. 230pp. 5⅜ × 8½. 22947-5 Pa. $4.00

PICTURE HISTORY OF THE NORMANDIE: With 190 Illustrations, Frank O. Braynard. Full story of legendary French ocean liner: Art Deco interiors, design innovations, furnishings, celebrities, maiden voyage, tragic fire, much more. Extensive text. 144pp. 8⅞ × 11¾. 25257-4 Pa. $9.95

THE FIRST AMERICAN COOKBOOK: A Facsimile of "American Cookery," 1796, Amelia Simmons. Facsimile of the first American-written cookbook published in the United States contains authentic recipes for colonial favorites—pumpkin pudding, winter squash pudding, spruce beer, Indian slapjacks, and more. Introductory Essay and Glossary of colonial cooking terms. 80pp. 5⅜ × 8½. 24710-4 Pa. $3.50

101 PUZZLES IN THOUGHT AND LOGIC, C. R. Wylie, Jr. Solve murders and robberies, find out which fishermen are liars, how a blind man could possibly identify a color—purely by your own reasoning! 107pp. 5⅜ × 8½. 20367-0 Pa. $2.00

THE BOOK OF WORLD-FAMOUS MUSIC—CLASSICAL, POPULAR AND FOLK, James J. Fuld. Revised and enlarged republication of landmark work in musico-bibliography. Full information about nearly 1,000 songs and compositions including first lines of music and lyrics. New supplement. Index. 800pp. 5⅜ × 8¼. 24857-7 Pa. $14.95

ANTHROPOLOGY AND MODERN LIFE, Franz Boas. Great anthropologist's classic treatise on race and culture. Introduction by Ruth Bunzel. Only inexpensive paperback edition. 255pp. 5⅜ × 8½. 25245-0 Pa. $5.95

THE TALE OF PETER RABBIT, Beatrix Potter. The inimitable Peter's terrifying adventure in Mr. McGregor's garden, with all 27 wonderful, full-color Potter illustrations. 55pp. 4¼ × 5½. (Available in U.S. only) 22827-4 Pa. $1.75

THREE PROPHETIC SCIENCE FICTION NOVELS, H. G. Wells. *When the Sleeper Wakes, A Story of the Days to Come* and *The Time Machine* (full version). 335pp. 5⅜ × 8½. (Available in U.S. only) 20605-X Pa. $5.95

APICIUS COOKERY AND DINING IN IMPERIAL ROME, edited and translated by Joseph Dommers Vehling. Oldest known cookbook in existence offers readers a clear picture of what foods Romans ate, how they prepared them, etc. 49 illustrations. 301pp. 6⅛ × 9¼. 23563-7 Pa. $6.00

SHAKESPEARE LEXICON AND QUOTATION DICTIONARY, Alexander Schmidt. Full definitions, locations, shades of meaning of every word in plays and poems. More than 50,000 exact quotations. 1,485pp. 6½ × 9¼. 22726-X, 22727-8 Pa., Two-vol. set $27.90

THE WORLD'S GREAT SPEECHES, edited by Lewis Copeland and Lawrence W. Lamm. Vast collection of 278 speeches from Greeks to 1970. Powerful and effective models; unique look at history. 842pp. 5⅜ × 8½. 20468-5 Pa. $10.95

THE BLUE FAIRY BOOK, Andrew Lang. The first, most famous collection, with many familiar tales: Little Red Riding Hood, Aladdin and the Wonderful Lamp, Puss in Boots, Sleeping Beauty, Hansel and Gretel, Rumpelstiltskin; 37 in all. 138 illustrations. 390pp. 5⅜ × 8½. 21437-0 Pa. $5.95

THE STORY OF THE CHAMPIONS OF THE ROUND TABLE, Howard Pyle. Sir Launcelot, Sir Tristram and Sir Percival in spirited adventures of love and triumph retold in Pyle's inimitable style. 50 drawings, 31 full-page. xviii + 329pp. 6½ × 9¼. 21883-X Pa. $6.95

AUDUBON AND HIS JOURNALS, Maria Audubon. Unmatched two-volume portrait of the great artist, naturalist and author contains his journals, an excellent biography by his granddaughter, expert annotations by the noted ornithologist, Dr. Elliott Coues, and 37 superb illustrations. Total of 1,200pp. 5⅜ × 8.
Vol. I 25143-8 Pa. $8.95
Vol. II 25144-6 Pa. $8.95

GREAT DINOSAUR HUNTERS AND THEIR DISCOVERIES, Edwin H. Colbert. Fascinating, lavishly illustrated chronicle of dinosaur research, 1820's to 1960. Achievements of Cope, Marsh, Brown, Buckland, Mantell, Huxley, many others. 384pp. 5¼ × 8¼. 24701-5 Pa. $6.95

THE TASTEMAKERS, Russell Lynes. Informal, illustrated social history of American taste 1850's–1950's. First popularized categories Highbrow, Lowbrow, Middlebrow. 129 illustrations. New (1979) afterword. 384pp. 6 × 9.
23993-4 Pa. $6.95

DOUBLE CROSS PURPOSES, Ronald A. Knox. A treasure hunt in the Scottish Highlands, an old map, unidentified corpse, surprise discoveries keep reader guessing in this cleverly intricate tale of financial skullduggery. 2 black-and-white maps. 320pp. 5⅜ × 8½. (Available in U.S. only) 25032-6 Pa. $5.95

AUTHENTIC VICTORIAN DECORATION AND ORNAMENTATION IN FULL COLOR: 46 Plates from "Studies in Design," Christopher Dresser. Superb full-color lithographs reproduced from rare original portfolio of a major Victorian designer. 48pp. 9¼ × 12¼. 25083-0 Pa. $7.95

PRIMITIVE ART, Franz Boas. Remains the best text ever prepared on subject, thoroughly discussing Indian, African, Asian, Australian, and, especially, Northern American primitive art. Over 950 illustrations show ceramics, masks, totem poles, weapons, textiles, paintings, much more. 376pp. 5⅜ × 8. 20025-6 Pa. $6.95

SIDELIGHTS ON RELATIVITY, Albert Einstein. Unabridged republication of two lectures delivered by the great physicist in 1920–21. *Ether and Relativity* and *Geometry and Experience*. Elegant ideas in non-mathematical form, accessible to intelligent layman. vi + 56pp. 5⅜ × 8½. 24511-X Pa. $2.95

THE WIT AND HUMOR OF OSCAR WILDE, edited by Alvin Redman. More than 1,000 ripostes, paradoxes, wisecracks: Work is the curse of the drinking classes, I can resist everything except temptation, etc. 258pp. 5⅜ × 8½. 20602-5 Pa. $3.95

ADVENTURES WITH A MICROSCOPE, Richard Headstrom. 59 adventures with clothing fibers, protozoa, ferns and lichens, roots and leaves, much more. 142 illustrations. 232pp. 5⅜ × 8½. 23471-1 Pa. $3.95

PLANTS OF THE BIBLE, Harold N. Moldenke and Alma L. Moldenke. Standard reference to all 230 plants mentioned in Scriptures. Latin name, biblical reference, uses, modern identity, much more. Unsurpassed encyclopedic resource for scholars, botanists, nature lovers, students of Bible. Bibliography. Indexes. 123 black-and-white illustrations. 384pp. 6 × 9. 25069-5 Pa. $8.95

FAMOUS AMERICAN WOMEN: A Biographical Dictionary from Colonial Times to the Present, Robert McHenry, ed. From Pocahontas to Rosa Parks, 1,035 distinguished American women documented in separate biographical entries. Accurate, up-to-date data, numerous categories, spans 400 years. Indices. 493pp. 6½ × 9¼. 24523-3 Pa. $9.95

THE FABULOUS INTERIORS OF THE GREAT OCEAN LINERS IN HISTORIC PHOTOGRAPHS, William H. Miller, Jr. Some 200 superb photographs capture exquisite interiors of world's great "floating palaces"—1890's to 1980's: *Titanic, Ile de France, Queen Elizabeth, United States, Europa,* more. Approx. 200 black-and-white photographs. Captions. Text. Introduction. 160pp. 8⅜ × 11¾. 24756-2 Pa. $9.95

THE GREAT LUXURY LINERS, 1927–1954: A Photographic Record, William H. Miller, Jr. Nostalgic tribute to heyday of ocean liners. 186 photos of Ile de France, Normandie, Leviathan, Queen Elizabeth, United States, many others. Interior and exterior views. Introduction. Captions. 160pp. 9 × 12. 24056-8 Pa. $9.95

A NATURAL HISTORY OF THE DUCKS, John Charles Phillips. Great landmark of ornithology offers complete detailed coverage of nearly 200 species and subspecies of ducks: gadwall, sheldrake, merganser, pintail, many more. 74 full-color plates, 102 black-and-white. Bibliography. Total of 1,920pp. 8⅜ × 11¼. 25141-1, 25142-X Cloth. Two-vol. set $100.00

THE SEAWEED HANDBOOK: An Illustrated Guide to Seaweeds from North Carolina to Canada, Thomas F. Lee. Concise reference covers 78 species. Scientific and common names, habitat, distribution, more. Finding keys for easy identification. 224pp. 5⅜ × 8½. 25215-9 Pa. $5.95

THE TEN BOOKS OF ARCHITECTURE: The 1755 Leoni Edition, Leon Battista Alberti. Rare classic helped introduce the glories of ancient architecture to the Renaissance. 68 black-and-white plates. 336pp. 8⅜ × 11¼. 25239-6 Pa. $14.95

MISS MACKENZIE, Anthony Trollope. Minor masterpieces by Victorian master unmasks many truths about life in 19th-century England. First inexpensive edition in years. 392pp. 5⅜ × 8½. 25201-9 Pa. $7.95

THE RIME OF THE ANCIENT MARINER, Gustave Doré, Samuel Taylor Coleridge. Dramatic engravings considered by many to be his greatest work. The terrifying space of the open sea, the storms and whirlpools of an unknown ocean, the ice of Antarctica, more—all rendered in a powerful, chilling manner. Full text. 38 plates. 77pp. 9¼ × 12. 22305-1 Pa. $4.95

THE EXPEDITIONS OF ZEBULON MONTGOMERY PIKE, Zebulon Montgomery Pike. Fascinating first-hand accounts (1805–6) of exploration of Mississippi River, Indian wars, capture by Spanish dragoons, much more. 1,088pp. 5⅜ × 8½. 25254-X, 25255-8 Pa. Two-vol. set $23.90

A CONCISE HISTORY OF PHOTOGRAPHY: Third Revised Edition, Helmut Gernsheim. Best one-volume history—camera obscura, photochemistry, daguerreotypes, evolution of cameras, film, more. Also artistic aspects—landscape, portraits, fine art, etc. 281 black-and-white photographs. 26 in color. 176pp. 8⅜ × 11¼. 25128-4 Pa. $12.95

THE DORÉ BIBLE ILLUSTRATIONS, Gustave Doré. 241 detailed plates from the Bible: the Creation scenes, Adam and Eve, Flood, Babylon, battle sequences, life of Jesus, etc. Each plate is accompanied by the verses from the King James version of the Bible. 241pp. 9 × 12. 23004-X Pa. $8.95

HUGGER-MUGGER IN THE LOUVRE, Elliot Paul. Second Homer Evans mystery-comedy. Theft at the Louvre involves sleuth in hilarious, madcap caper. "A knockout."—Books. 336pp. 5⅜ × 8½. 25185-3 Pa. $5.95

FLATLAND, E. A. Abbott. Intriguing and enormously popular science-fiction classic explores the complexities of trying to survive as a two-dimensional being in a three-dimensional world. Amusingly illustrated by the author. 16 illustrations. 103pp. 5⅜ × 8½. 20001-9 Pa. $2.00

THE HISTORY OF THE LEWIS AND CLARK EXPEDITION, Meriwether Lewis and William Clark, edited by Elliott Coues. Classic edition of Lewis and Clark's day-by-day journals that later became the basis for U.S. claims to Oregon and the West. Accurate and invaluable geographical, botanical, biological, meteorological and anthropological material. Total of 1,508pp. 5⅜ × 8½. 21268-8, 21269-6, 21270-X Pa. Three-vol. set $25.50

LANGUAGE, TRUTH AND LOGIC, Alfred J. Ayer. Famous, clear introduction to Vienna, Cambridge schools of Logical Positivism. Role of philosophy, elimination of metaphysics, nature of analysis, etc. 160pp. 5⅜ × 8½. (Available in U.S. and Canada only) 20010-8 Pa. $2.95

MATHEMATICS FOR THE NONMATHEMATICIAN, Morris Kline. Detailed, college-level treatment of mathematics in cultural and historical context, with numerous exercises. For liberal arts students. Preface. Recommended Reading Lists. Tables. Index. Numerous black-and-white figures. xvi + 641pp. 5⅜ × 8½. 24823-2 Pa. $11.95

28 SCIENCE FICTION STORIES, H. G. Wells. Novels, *Star Begotten* and *Men Like Gods,* plus 26 short stories: "Empire of the Ants," "A Story of the Stone Age," "The Stolen Bacillus," "In the Abyss," etc. 915pp. 5⅜ × 8½. (Available in U.S. only) 20265-8 Cloth. $10.95

HANDBOOK OF PICTORIAL SYMBOLS, Rudolph Modley. 3,250 signs and symbols, many systems in full; official or heavy commercial use. Arranged by subject. Most in Pictorial Archive series. 143pp. 8⅛ × 11. 23357-X Pa. $5.95

INCIDENTS OF TRAVEL IN YUCATAN, John L. Stephens. Classic (1843) exploration of jungles of Yucatan, looking for evidences of Maya civilization. Travel adventures, Mexican and Indian culture, etc. Total of 669pp. 5⅜ × 8½. 20926-1, 20927-X Pa., Two-vol. set $9.90

CATALOG OF DOVER BOOKS

DEGAS: An Intimate Portrait, Ambroise Vollard. Charming, anecdotal memoir by famous art dealer of one of the greatest 19th-century French painters. 14 black-and-white illustrations. Introduction by Harold L. Van Doren. 96pp. 5⅜ × 8½.
25131-4 Pa. $3.95

PERSONAL NARRATIVE OF A PILGRIMAGE TO ALMANDINAH AND MECCAH, Richard Burton. Great travel classic by remarkably colorful personality. Burton, disguised as a Moroccan, visited sacred shrines of Islam, narrowly escaping death. 47 illustrations. 959pp. 5⅜ × 8½. 21217-3, 21218-1 Pa., Two-vol. set $17.90

PHRASE AND WORD ORIGINS, A. H. Holt. Entertaining, reliable, modern study of more than 1,200 colorful words, phrases, origins and histories. Much unexpected information. 254pp. 5⅜ × 8½. 20758-7 Pa. $4.95

THE RED THUMB MARK, R. Austin Freeman. In this first Dr. Thorndyke case, the great scientific detective draws fascinating conclusions from the nature of a single fingerprint. Exciting story, authentic science. 320pp. 5⅜ × 8½. (Available in U.S. only) 25210-8 Pa. $5.95

AN EGYPTIAN HIEROGLYPHIC DICTIONARY, E. A. Wallis Budge. Monumental work containing about 25,000 words or terms that occur in texts ranging from 3000 B.C. to 600 A.D. Each entry consists of a transliteration of the word, the word in hieroglyphs, and the meaning in English. 1,314pp. 6⅜ × 10.
23615-3, 23616-1 Pa., Two-vol. set $27.90

THE COMPLEAT STRATEGYST: Being a Primer on the Theory of Games of Strategy, J. D. Williams. Highly entertaining classic describes, with many illustrated examples, how to select best strategies in conflict situations. Prefaces. Appendices. xvi + 268pp. 5⅜ × 8½. 25101-2 Pa. $5.95

THE ROAD TO OZ, L. Frank Baum. Dorothy meets the Shaggy Man, little Button-Bright and the Rainbow's beautiful daughter in this delightful trip to the magical Land of Oz. 272pp. 5⅜ × 8. 25208-6 Pa. $4.95

POINT AND LINE TO PLANE, Wassily Kandinsky. Seminal exposition of role of point, line, other elements in non-objective painting. Essential to understanding 20th-century art. 127 illustrations. 192pp. 6½ × 9¼. 23808-3 Pa. $4.50

LADY ANNA, Anthony Trollope. Moving chronicle of Countess Lovel's bitter struggle to win for herself and daughter Anna their rightful rank and fortune—perhaps at cost of sanity itself. 384pp. 5⅜ × 8½. 24669-8 Pa. $6.95

EGYPTIAN MAGIC, E. A. Wallis Budge. Sums up all that is known about magic in Ancient Egypt: the role of magic in controlling the gods, powerful amulets that warded off evil spirits, scarabs of immortality, use of wax images, formulas and spells, the secret name, much more. 253pp. 5⅜ × 8½. 22681-6 Pa. $4.00

THE DANCE OF SIVA, Ananda Coomaraswamy. Preeminent authority unfolds the vast metaphysic of India: the revelation of her art, conception of the universe, social organization, etc. 27 reproductions of art masterpieces. 192pp. 5⅜ × 8½.
24817-8 Pa. $5.95

CHRISTMAS CUSTOMS AND TRADITIONS, Clement A. Miles. Origin, evolution, significance of religious, secular practices. Caroling, gifts, yule logs, much more. Full, scholarly yet fascinating; non-sectarian. 400pp. 5⅜ × 8½.
23354-5 Pa. $6.50

THE HUMAN FIGURE IN MOTION, Eadweard Muybridge. More than 4,500 stopped-action photos, in action series, showing undraped men, women, children jumping, lying down, throwing, sitting, wrestling, carrying, etc. 390pp. 7⅞ × 10⅝.
20204-6 Cloth. $19.95

THE MAN WHO WAS THURSDAY, Gilbert Keith Chesterton. Witty, fast-paced novel about a club of anarchists in turn-of-the-century London. Brilliant social, religious, philosophical speculations. 128pp. 5⅜ × 8½. 25121-7 Pa. $3.95

A CEZANNE SKETCHBOOK: Figures, Portraits, Landscapes and Still Lifes, Paul Cezanne. Great artist experiments with tonal effects, light, mass, other qualities in over 100 drawings. A revealing view of developing master painter, precursor of Cubism. 102 black-and-white illustrations. 144pp. 8¾ × 6⅜. 24790-2 Pa. $5.95

AN ENCYCLOPEDIA OF BATTLES: Accounts of Over 1,560 Battles from 1479 B.C. to the Present, David Eggenberger. Presents essential details of every major battle in recorded history, from the first battle of Megiddo in 1479 B.C. to Grenada in 1984. List of Battle Maps. New Appendix covering the years 1967–1984. Index. 99 illustrations. 544pp. 6½ × 9¼. 24913-1 Pa. $14.95

AN ETYMOLOGICAL DICTIONARY OF MODERN ENGLISH, Ernest Weekley. Richest, fullest work, by foremost British lexicographer. Detailed word histories. Inexhaustible. Total of 856pp. 6½ × 9¼.
21873-2, 21874-0 Pa., Two-vol. set $17.00

WEBSTER'S AMERICAN MILITARY BIOGRAPHIES, edited by Robert McHenry. Over 1,000 figures who shaped 3 centuries of American military history. Detailed biographies of Nathan Hale, Douglas MacArthur, Mary Hallaren, others. Chronologies of engagements, more. Introduction. Addenda. 1,033 entries in alphabetical order. xi + 548pp. 6½ × 9¼. (Available in U.S. only)
24758-9 Pa. $11.95

LIFE IN ANCIENT EGYPT, Adolf Erman. Detailed older account, with much not in more recent books: domestic life, religion, magic, medicine, commerce, and whatever else needed for complete picture. Many illustrations. 597pp. 5⅜ × 8½.
22632-8 Pa. $8.50

HISTORIC COSTUME IN PICTURES, Braun & Schneider. Over 1,450 costumed figures shown, covering a wide variety of peoples: kings, emperors, nobles, priests, servants, soldiers, scholars, townsfolk, peasants, merchants, courtiers, cavaliers, and more. 256pp. 8⅜ × 11¼. 23150-X Pa. $7.95

THE NOTEBOOKS OF LEONARDO DA VINCI, edited by J. P. Richter. Extracts from manuscripts reveal great genius; on painting, sculpture, anatomy, sciences, geography, etc. Both Italian and English. 186 ms. pages reproduced, plus 500 additional drawings, including studies for *Last Supper, Sforza* monument, etc. 860pp. 7⅞ × 10¾. (Available in U.S. only) 22572-0, 22573-9 Pa., Two-vol. set $25.90

THE ART NOUVEAU STYLE BOOK OF ALPHONSE MUCHA: All 72 Plates from "Documents Decoratifs" in Original Color, Alphonse Mucha. Rare copyright-free design portfolio by high priest of Art Nouveau. Jewelry, wallpaper, stained glass, furniture, figure studies, plant and animal motifs, etc. Only complete one-volume edition. 80pp. 9⅜ × 12¼. 24044-4 Pa. $8.95

ANIMALS: 1,419 COPYRIGHT-FREE ILLUSTRATIONS OF MAMMALS, BIRDS, FISH, INSECTS, ETC., edited by Jim Harter. Clear wood engravings present, in extremely lifelike poses, over 1,000 species of animals. One of the most extensive pictorial sourcebooks of its kind. Captions. Index. 284pp. 9 × 12. 23766-4 Pa. $9.95

OBELISTS FLY HIGH, C. Daly King. Masterpiece of American detective fiction, long out of print, involves murder on a 1935 transcontinental flight—"a very thrilling story"—NY Times. Unabridged and unaltered republication of the edition published by William Collins Sons & Co. Ltd., London, 1935. 288pp. 5⅜ × 8½. (Available in U.S. only) 25036-9 Pa. $4.95

VICTORIAN AND EDWARDIAN FASHION: A Photographic Survey, Alison Gernsheim. First fashion history completely illustrated by contemporary photographs. Full text plus 235 photos, 1840-1914, in which many celebrities appear. 240pp. 6½ × 9¼. 24205-6 Pa. $6.00

THE ART OF THE FRENCH ILLUSTRATED BOOK, 1700-1914, Gordon N. Ray. Over 630 superb book illustrations by Fragonard, Delacroix, Daumier, Doré, Grandville, Manet, Mucha, Steinlen, Toulouse-Lautrec and many others. Preface. Introduction. 633 halftones. Indices of artists, authors & titles, binders and provenances. Appendices. Bibliography. 608pp. 8⅜ × 11¼. 25086-5 Pa. $24.95

THE WONDERFUL WIZARD OF OZ, L. Frank Baum. Facsimile in full color of America's finest children's classic. 143 illustrations by W. W. Denslow. 267pp. 5⅜ × 8½. 20691-2 Pa. $5.95

FRONTIERS OF MODERN PHYSICS: New Perspectives on Cosmology, Relativity, Black Holes and Extraterrestrial Intelligence, Tony Rothman, et al. For the intelligent layman. Subjects include: cosmological models of the universe; black holes; the neutrino; the search for extraterrestrial intelligence. Introduction. 46 black-and-white illustrations. 192pp. 5⅜ × 8½. 24587-X Pa. $6.95

THE FRIENDLY STARS, Martha Evans Martin & Donald Howard Menzel. Classic text marshalls the stars together in an engaging, non-technical survey, presenting them as sources of beauty in night sky. 23 illustrations. Foreword. 2 star charts. Index. 147pp. 5⅜ × 8½. 21099-5 Pa. $3.50

FADS AND FALLACIES IN THE NAME OF SCIENCE, Martin Gardner. Fair, witty appraisal of cranks, quacks, and quackeries of science and pseudoscience: hollow earth, Velikovsky, orgone energy, Dianetics, flying saucers, Bridey Murphy, food and medical fads, etc. Revised, expanded In the Name of Science. "A very able and even-tempered presentation."—The New Yorker. 363pp. 5⅜ × 8. 20394-8 Pa. $5.95

ANCIENT EGYPT: ITS CULTURE AND HISTORY, J. E Manchip White. From pre-dynastics through Ptolemies: society, history, political structure, religion, daily life, literature, cultural heritage. 48 plates. 217pp. 5⅜ × 8½. 22548-8 Pa. $4.95

SIR HARRY HOTSPUR OF HUMBLETHWAITE, Anthony Trollope. Incisive, unconventional psychological study of a conflict between a wealthy baronet, his idealistic daughter, and their scapegrace cousin. The 1870 novel in its first inexpensive edition in years. 250pp. 5⅜ × 8½. 24953-0 Pa. $4.95

LASERS AND HOLOGRAPHY, Winston E. Kock. Sound introduction to burgeoning field, expanded (1981) for second edition. Wave patterns, coherence, lasers, diffraction, zone plates, properties of holograms, recent advances. 84 illustrations. 160pp. 5⅜ × 8¼. (Except in United Kingdom) 24041-X Pa. $3.50

INTRODUCTION TO ARTIFICIAL INTELLIGENCE: SECOND, ENLARGED EDITION, Philip C. Jackson, Jr. Comprehensive survey of artificial intelligence—the study of how machines (computers) can be made to act intelligently. Includes introductory and advanced material. Extensive notes updating the main text. 132 black-and-white illustrations. 512pp. 5⅜ × 8½. 24864-X Pa. $8.95

HISTORY OF INDIAN AND INDONESIAN ART, Ananda K. Coomaraswamy. Over 400 illustrations illuminate classic study of Indian art from earliest Harappa finds to early 20th century. Provides philosophical, religious and social insights. 304pp. 6⅜ × 9⅜. 25005-9 Pa. $8.95

THE GOLEM, Gustav Meyrink. Most famous supernatural novel in modern European literature, set in Ghetto of Old Prague around 1890. Compelling story of mystical experiences, strange transformations, profound terror. 13 black-and-white illustrations. 224pp. 5⅜ × 8½. (Available in U.S. only) 25025-3 Pa. $5.95

ARMADALE, Wilkie Collins. Third great mystery novel by the author of *The Woman in White* and *The Moonstone*. Original magazine version with 40 illustrations. 597pp. 5⅜ × 8½. 23429-0 Pa. $7.95

PICTORIAL ENCYCLOPEDIA OF HISTORIC ARCHITECTURAL PLANS, DETAILS AND ELEMENTS: With 1,880 Line Drawings of Arches, Domes, Doorways, Facades, Gables, Windows, etc., John Theodore Haneman. Sourcebook of inspiration for architects, designers, others. Bibliography. Captions. 141pp. 9 × 12. 24605-1 Pa. $6.95

BENCHLEY LOST AND FOUND, Robert Benchley. Finest humor from early 30's, about pet peeves, child psychologists, post office and others. Mostly unavailable elsewhere. 73 illustrations by Peter Arno and others. 183pp. 5⅜ × 8½. 22410-4 Pa. $3.95

ERTÉ GRAPHICS, Erté. Collection of striking color graphics: *Seasons, Alphabet, Numerals, Aces* and *Precious Stones*. 50 plates, including 4 on covers. 48pp. 9⅜ × 12¼. 23580-7 Pa. $6.95

THE JOURNAL OF HENRY D. THOREAU, edited by Bradford Torrey, F. H. Allen. Complete reprinting of 14 volumes, 1837–61, over two million words; the sourcebooks for *Walden*, etc. Definitive. All original sketches, plus 75 photographs. 1,804pp. 8½ × 12¼. 20312-3, 20313-1 Cloth., Two-vol. set $80.00

CASTLES: THEIR CONSTRUCTION AND HISTORY, Sidney Toy. Traces castle development from ancient roots. Nearly 200 photographs and drawings illustrate moats, keeps, baileys, many other features. Caernarvon, Dover Castles, Hadrian's Wall, Tower of London, dozens more. 256pp. 5⅜ × 8¼. 24898-4 Pa. $5.95

CATALOG OF DOVER BOOKS

AMERICAN CLIPPER SHIPS: 1833–1858, Octavius T. Howe & Frederick C. Matthews. Fully-illustrated, encyclopedic review of 352 clipper ships from the period of America's greatest maritime supremacy. Introduction. 109 halftones. 5 black-and-white line illustrations. Index. Total of 928pp. 5⅜ × 8½.
25115-2, 25116-0 Pa., Two-vol. set $17.90

TOWARDS A NEW ARCHITECTURE, Le Corbusier. Pioneering manifesto by great architect, near legendary founder of "International School." Technical and aesthetic theories, views on industry, economics, relation of form to function, "mass-production spirit," much more. Profusely illustrated. Unabridged translation of 13th French edition. Introduction by Frederick Etchells. 320pp. 6⅛ × 9¼. (Available in U.S. only)
25023-7 Pa. $8.95

THE BOOK OF KELLS, edited by Blanche Cirker. Inexpensive collection of 32 full-color, full-page plates from the greatest illuminated manuscript of the Middle Ages, painstakingly reproduced from rare facsimile edition. Publisher's Note. Captions. 32pp. 9⅜ × 12¼.
24345-1 Pa. $4.50

BEST SCIENCE FICTION STORIES OF H. G. WELLS, H. G. Wells. Full novel *The Invisible Man*, plus 17 short stories: "The Crystal Egg," "Aepyornis Island," "The Strange Orchid," etc. 303pp. 5⅜ × 8½. (Available in U.S. only)
21531-8 Pa. $4.95

AMERICAN SAILING SHIPS: Their Plans and History, Charles G. Davis. Photos, construction details of schooners, frigates, clippers, other sailcraft of 18th to early 20th centuries—plus entertaining discourse on design, rigging, nautical lore, much more. 137 black-and-white illustrations. 240pp. 6⅛ × 9¼.
24658-2 Pa. $5.95

ENTERTAINING MATHEMATICAL PUZZLES, Martin Gardner. Selection of author's favorite conundrums involving arithmetic, money, speed, etc., with lively commentary. Complete solutions. 112pp. 5⅜ × 8½.   25211-6 Pa. $2.95

THE WILL TO BELIEVE, HUMAN IMMORTALITY, William James. Two books bound together. Effect of irrational on logical, and arguments for human immortality. 402pp. 5⅜ × 8½.   20291-7 Pa. $7.50

THE HAUNTED MONASTERY and THE CHINESE MAZE MURDERS, Robert Van Gulik. 2 full novels by Van Gulik continue adventures of Judge Dee and his companions. An evil Taoist monastery, seemingly supernatural events; overgrown topiary maze that hides strange crimes. Set in 7th-century China. 27 illustrations. 328pp. 5⅜ × 8½.   23502-5 Pa. $5.00

CELEBRATED CASES OF JUDGE DEE (DEE GOONG AN), translated by Robert Van Gulik. Authentic 18th-century Chinese detective novel; Dee and associates solve three interlocked cases. Led to Van Gulik's own stories with same characters. Extensive introduction. 9 illustrations. 237pp. 5⅜ × 8½.
23337-5 Pa. $4.95

Prices subject to change without notice.
Available at your book dealer or write for free catalog to Dept. GI, Dover Publications, Inc., 31 East 2nd St., Mineola, N.Y. 11501. Dover publishes more than 175 books each year on science, elementary and advanced mathematics, biology, music, art, literary history, social sciences and other areas.